GOING GLOBAL

An Introduction to International Marketing

PEARSON
Prentice Hall

FORUM FOR INTERNATIONAL
TRADE TRAINING

FORUM POUR LA FORMATION EN
COMMERCE INTERNATIONAL

FORUM FOR INTERNATIONAL TRADE TRAINING

FITT

FORUM POUR LA FORMATION EN COMMERCE INTERNATIONAL

Join an Elite Group of Professionals

Certified International Trade Professional

"are opening doors to the world"

Set yourself apart with the Certified International Trade Professional (C.I.T.P.) designation.

The C.I.T.P. is the only professional designation of its kind for **international trade practitioners**. The attainment and use of the C.I.T.P. designation is proof that you have met rigorous standards established by a recognized certifying body, the **Forum for International Trade Training (FITT)**.

Differentiate yourself as an entrepreneur or within the business community by holding this credential of excellence.

C.I.T.P.—when these four letters follow your name:
- Customers and colleagues know they are dealing with a knowledgeable professional who adheres to a Code of Ethics
- Employers know that you have solid international business skills and experience, and the credentials to prove it
- Your validated education and experience will set you apart in the competitive market
- You know that you've reached a level of achievement that you can be proud of
- You know that you've met national standards and certification in a growing, exciting field

As a C.I.T.P., you will:
- Be highly respected by your colleagues
- Acquire more credibility in your field
- Increase your career opportunities
- Help strengthen the image of international trade as a profession

For your employer, certification will:
- Establish a benchmark for others
- Set a hiring standard for new staff
- Increase credibility with customers
- Differentiate their international team from the competition

Certification requirements:
To qualify for the C.I.T.P. designation, candidates must satisfy both educational and practical international trade work experience.

To find out more about the C.I.T.P. designation:
Contact FITT, or visit www.fitt.ca. FITT is committed to providing quality international trade training and certification. C.I.T.P.—the credential of excellence in international trade since 1997.

Table of Contents

List of Figures

Acknowledgments

Forum for International Trade Training (FITT) would like to express its appreciation and thanks to the many professional industry contributors and supporters in the development and publication of this workshop material.

In particular, FITT wishes to recognize the contributions of Robert Savard, for his work in the development of the original workshop content, and John MacDonald and David Wallace for their role in updating the present revised edition.

FITT would also like to recognize the contribution of Leroy Lowe for his role as chair of the work plan committee and the committee members: Dov Bercovici, Charles Donley, Gaëlle Gagné, Désirée Sauvé, Robert Savard and Rachelle Soulière. For their contribution as reviewers of the workshop content, FITT also appreciates the support of Robert Lajoie, Javier Lopez and Leroy Lowe.

In addition, FITT also wishes to thank Naheed Rizvi for her contribution to the content update and publishing processes and to recognize the rest of the publishing team:

Editing: Jan Fedorowicz and McE Galbreath (The Summit Group Inc.)

Production: Veracity Consulting Inc.

Printing: Doculink International Inc.

This project is funded in part by the Government of Canada. FITT is grateful for both the professional and financial support of Industry Canada and Team Canada Inc in developing the *Going Global* workshop series.

Introduction

Workshop objectives

- Design a successful international marketing strategy for a company's products or services using the information from this workshop.

- Develop an international marketing plan applying the global marketing information from this workshop.

- Access current online information relevant to a business by using the web sites recommended throughout this workshop.

The marketing function and related activities in an enterprise, small or large, ensure that an enterprise gets information from its customers, develops and markets the services to satisfy their needs, and gets feedback on their satisfaction levels.

Marketing represents the interface between an enterprise and its customers, but it does not operate on its own – it interacts with other functions. For example, marketing, finance, accounting and production determine price levels; marketing and human resources develop customer service policies; and marketing and public relations create and support the image of an enterprise.

Marketing can be summarized as the function that encompasses most activities between the producer of a good or the supplier of a service and the consumer. It is also a set of business development activities that start with the consumer from whose needs the business gets its service ideas and to whom it will sell its services at a profit.

A Canadian marketing textbook has this definition of the process:

Marketers, while keeping in mind the various roles in the marketplace, must keep in mind that their principal task is to offer customers a product or service that will produce satisfaction. Marketing is the process of satisfying customer needs and wants through an exchange process.[1]

This workshop introduces you to the role of marketing in the pursuit of international business opportunities. One of the workshop's major benefits is that you will be provided with the basic knowledge and skills to start the development of an international marketing plan – based on the template presented at the end of your *Participant Guide*.

The need to train and prepare Canadian exporters motivated the founders of the Forum for International Trade Training (FITT) to create, in 1992, what is now recognized as Canada's centre for international trade training.

---

[1] Montrose S. Sommers and James G. Barnes, *Fundamentals of Marketing*, 9th Canadian Ed. (Toronto: McGraw-Hill Ryerson, 2001), p.6.

This three-hour workshop on international marketing is a good beginning to understanding this complex aspect of your business. While much of your *Participant Guide* will be presented during the workshop, not all of it will be presented in detail. It is recommended that participants pursue further training and preparation. This easy-to-read guide can be used as a handy reference whenever needed.

The contents of this workshop were assembled from the extensive curriculum of the FITTskills material entitled *International Marketing* and from the web sites of *ExportSource, Strategis, Export Your Services: Take a World View* and others. In addition, there are numerous references to a wide range of sources of assistance, all of which will be instrumental in ensuring that you are in the best position to be *Going Global.*

How to use this workbook

While this workbook is not intended to be an encyclopedia of international marketing, it does cover many of the essential points to consider on this vast subject. It has also been designed as a quick reference guide for later use.

Therefore, numerous references are made to well-known and reliable sources of information and you are encouraged to complement this workshop with some research of your own.

Tips, suggestions, and comments are also made and your attention drawn to specific subjects.

Throughout the guide various web sites are suggested as references or as sources of further information. These web sites are up-to-date as of the time of writing. The Internet is a very fluid medium, however: information comes and goes; new web sites appear and disappear. FITT hopes that the sites referred to will last for some time, but there are no guarantees on the Internet. The sites are well documented in the text and complete addresses are given for easy access. If and when the web sites are revised and changed, participants should use the root address to access the site and then do a search for the material being sought. If there is no search facility at the site and the menus do not make it possible to find the required material, then go back to using a good search engine and you will most likely find the information you are looking for.

Get to know some good search engines such as **www.google.ca** or **www.google.com**, which operate in English and French, though there are many others as well. **www.goo.ne.jp** is a good Japanese search engine that also operates with English search queries. It is useful for the Japanese market, Canada's largest offshore trading partner.

There are also some metasearch engines, which search several search engines at the same time. One of these is Copernic Basic Agent, which can be downloaded free from **www.copernic.com**.

Students and international trade practitioners should make an effort to maintain their information sources, as they are vital to business intelligence. After reviewing recommended sites they should be bookmarked and refreshed regularly. Key intelligence sources are the currency of the new global reality.

Libraries are also useful. Most major cities will have a library with a good business section. In addition, public libraries often have business databases that can be used for free at the library. Outside the library, such databases may not be available online or may require a hefty subscription charge to access them. Universities and colleges also have good library resources and these are often available to local businesses and the general public.

The workshop section of this guide is followed by a condensed information section on Sources of Assistance, a Glossary, additional information on Incoterms, as well as an Index.

At the end of the guide there is also a Case Study. There are questions relating to the Case Study and your firm at the end of each chapter and the answers to these questions can be found in an Appendix at the end of this guide.

1. The Principles of Marketing

Objectives

The objectives for this chapter are as follows:

- **Identify the basic marketing principles a company needs to successfully market its products abroad.**

- **Explain the marketing process by which a company can successfully identify, anticipate and satisfy customer requirements.**

- **Discuss the marketing mix necessary to create an effective marketing plan for a company.**

- **Explain the key functions that a marketing department must be able to undertake to service customers abroad.**

1.1 Selling vs. marketing

A simple definition of the difference between a sales-oriented organization and a marketing-oriented organization is that:

- a sales-oriented company will "sell" the product it has: its sales force will promote the benefits and the features of the product;

- a company oriented to marketing will first find out what the customer wants or needs and then make a product that addresses those wants and needs.

The following is an interesting international marketing example. During the early 1970s, the British Columbia Council of Forest Industries (COFI) started a 2x4 sales program in Japan. This was a promotional effort, to "market" the idea for building Japanese style houses, using the North American platform frame (2x4) construction system. They were able to do this because there were already several Japanese housing companies who were very interested in platform frame construction, and the program catered to those needs. The program was successful and for some time now a substantial percentage of wood frame homes in Japan have been built with the 2x4 platform frame system, using Canadian 2x4 dimension lumber.

A majority of more than one million housing starts per year in Japan are actually concrete apartments. The other wood frame houses in Japan, other than 2x4 and proprietary prefab systems, have usually been built using a traditional post and beam system called *zairai koho*. Sometime after the successful initiation of the 2x4 platform frame program, the BC lumber industry noticed that there was a strong demand in Japan for post and beam lumber for traditional Japanese *zairai koho* homes. The industry started several marketing efforts to use BC lumber sawn to traditional Japanese sizes, mostly a variety of square lumber sizes. Though these traditional Japanese lumber sizes had always been produced domestically, the effort to market Canadian products with the same specifications was also successful.

A similar approach to developing customer awareness, customer acceptance and consumer interest is now being pursued in the Chinese marketplace, particularly Shanghai. The Chinese marketplace does not have a tradition of single-family wood frame houses as Japan does. Most of the wood frame houses built so far are in housing compounds where they are rented to expatriate business people. Canadian business people see potential for the future, however, because concrete houses will have to be heavier to meet the energy efficient standards set by the Chinese government. The river delta where Shanghai is located has very soft soil, so heavy concrete houses will require expensive pilings. By contrast, the 2x4 wood frame houses are much lighter and the industry feels that theses houses will be attractive both in terms of cost and aesthetics.[2]

These and other examples of the interplay of product development and marketing suggest that if you are not truly customer-oriented, you are not even in the game!

> *"The aim of marketing is to make selling unnecessary."*
> *Peter Drucker*

1.2   What is marketing?

> *To succeed, marketers must know the customer in a context including the competition, government policy and regulation, and the broader economic, social, and political macro forces that shape the evolution of markets. In global marketing, this may mean working closely with home-country government trade negotiators and other officials and industry competitors to gain access to a target-country market.[3]*

For more detail on marketing, together with a diagnostic tool, see the Strategis web site and then type Steps to Competitiveness in the search box.

www.strategis.gc.ca

Whatever the specifics of the definition, most approaches to marketing start by recognizing that marketing is the part of a business involving direct communication between the company and the customer.

Communication is a two-way street. Those who think of marketing only in terms of advertising and selling should recall that those activities primarily involve communicating a company's messages to the customer. Another even more important part of marketing is to provide for communication in the other direction, from the customer back to the company. In fact, marketing starts by attempting to discover who the customer is, what the customer wants and how the company can best go about providing it. And the very best marketing will also include ongoing client tracking by which a company can continuously monitor customer reactions to its products, services and messages.

---

[2]   Don Cayo, "Builders have B.C. timber in the frame", *The Vancouver Sun*, June 17th, 2004, p. D6

[3]   J. Keegan, *Global Marketing Management*, 7th ed., (Upper Saddle River, NJ: Prentice Hall, 2002), p.3.

In the *Going Global* workshop, *An Introduction to International Market Research*, there is a discussion about how market research is used to gather information about potential customers: who they are, what they need, what they believe and what they are prepared to buy. This type of information is useful in shaping messages that convince potential customers to buy. It is also vital in designing the kinds of products and services that customers need. And it can help design a business so that it can profitably serve, satisfy and keep customers. Market research forms the strategic central core of a business, influencing everything from product/service research and development through production/delivery to after-sales follow-up and service. And, building upon market research, marketing is the way a company tells its potential customers that it understands them and acts to satisfy their needs and concerns.

For example, if market research suggests that a firm's customers are concerned about timely delivery, the company should reorganize its order-processing, handling and distribution system to ensure that its products or services are delivered on time and ahead of the competition. Once such changes are made, the company can modify its marketing by including sales messages that draw attention to its abilities in timely delivery.

Companies should never claim to be able to satisfy a customer's requirements if they cannot do so. Firms that think they can serve customers by relying on advertising and promotion alone are taking a huge risk. Customers are too sophisticated today to be satisfied by clever marketing messages that are not backed by actual practice. Exaggerated claims will only hurt the company's credibility and impair its long-term prospects.

Promotional activities – including advertising, public relations, publicity and selling – are important, but they are only useful in helping to establish one part of the relationship with the customer. In fact, it is useful to think of the moment a sale is closed as the moment when the door to the relationship is opened.

The sale is not the end of the marketing process. Instead, it provides a company with the opportunity to demonstrate that it can satisfy the customer's requirements. If it does so successfully – by delivering what the customer wants, providing after-sales service and monitoring customer satisfaction – it is more likely that the firm will be invited back for repeat business.

In their marketing efforts, today's companies are just as interested in maintaining their existing client base as they are in expanding into new markets. It takes less effort to reinforce the convictions of someone who has already been convinced than it does to persuade someone to invest in a brand new commercial relationship.

Comprehensive and accurate market research provides the information needed to modify a firm's products and services to truly meet customer needs. It can help to establish appropriate price levels and other terms of sale. In addition, it provides a firm with the direction it needs to tackle a host of other issues, including identifying, creating and managing markets, cultural sensitivities, advertising, customized promotional and sales techniques, and after-sales service.

Marketing is a complex, multidimensional process. It includes:

- knowing customers and their industry;

- understanding customer needs;

- evaluating the company's ability to satisfy those needs;

- modifying the product, service or process to better match what the customer wants;

- informing customers that the firm can satisfy their needs;

- facilitating the purchase of the product or service;

- delivery;

- after-sales service;

- monitoring satisfaction;

- maintaining effective internal communications, linking all levels of the organization to ensure that customer requirements are understood on an ongoing basis; and

- using customer reactions to improve the product, service or process.

The key to success in all of these activities is to focus on satisfying the customer.

Figure 1: Marketing is more than...

Knowing the customer	Companies can spend a lot of effort getting to know who their customers are. Some of these efforts can become intrusive and self-defeating. Unless they turn this activity into a genuine understanding of what customers want and how best to deliver it, the effort is wasted.
Products	A brilliant product portfolio can still drive a firm to bankruptcy unless the product represents what customers want, when they want it, where they want it, at a price they are willing to pay. It is not true that "if you build a better mousetrap, the world will beat a path to your door."
Advertising	Clever messages without an ability to deliver the goods will only undermine credibility without satisfying any of a company's basic challenges. Advertising is no substitute for solving product, process or service problems.
Selling	A focus on selling in isolation from the other elements of the marketing process will only lead to customer resistance and diminishing returns from the effort.
Service	Providing peripheral or unneeded services will not satisfy customers; it will only lead to added costs. In focusing on being excessively friendly, sending greeting cards at Christmas or providing cups of coffee to clients, companies can easily lose sight of what the customer really wants from them.

1.3 Elements of marketing

Marketing is a complex activity involving the effective integration of a number of basic activities. Marketers often talk about four, in particular:

1. **Product planning and development** – offering the right product or service to the right market.

2. **Place distribution and delivery** – making sure that the product or service is delivered to customers at the right time and in the right place.

3. **Pricing strategy** – ensuring that the price charged matches the value customers perceive.

4. **Promotion** – advertising, sales, public relations; persuading customers that you have what they need.

These activities are referred to as the "four P's" (product, place, price and promotion). Taken together, they are also called the "marketing mix." Each marketing strategy will involve a slightly different blend of these elements with their relative proportions determined by the specific nature of the business. For example, a company selling agricultural commodities will emphasize timely delivery ("place") at a competitive price in its marketing, while a firm specializing in alarm systems may choose to emphasize features and reliability ("product") instead of place or price.

Sometimes, companies make serious errors in the marketing mix they choose. A controversial example came to light when it was revealed that a contact lens manufacturer had marketed the same lenses to different customer groups. At one end of the spectrum, the lenses were presented as high quality and durable products for which a premium price was expected. At the other end, the lenses were marketed as disposable after a few uses and therefore inexpensive. The same product was offered, but with a radically different marketing mix. What seemed like a clever marketing strategy backfired on the manufacturer when it became public.

The activities included in the marketing mix are under the control of the marketer or marketing department. A slightly broader way of looking at marketing is to think of all the elements involved in the process, not just those under the company's control (see Figure 2). The challenge becomes one of integrating all of these elements into a comprehensive and effective marketing strategy.

Figure 2: The building blocks of marketing

Market	The market is an aggregate of all existing or potential customers that a company might conceivably address with its products or services. Markets typically experience trends: they can grow, contract or evolve under the impact of demographic and social changes, technological progress, macroeconomic performance or regulatory and legal changes.
Customers	Customers are the individuals who actually do the buying. Not all customers within a market are motivated by the same needs or values. Groups of customers sharing similar characteristics make up market segments. Even within a segment, individual customers may display unique behaviour to which companies may also need to be sensitive.
Product or Service	Companies are in business to make a profit by providing a product or service that customers want or need and for which they are willing to pay. Establishing what customers really want and then making sure that the company provides it is key to marketing success.
Value	Value is what companies create for their customers. It is the customers themselves, acting through the market, that determine what goods, services or processes they find valuable. Value is a composite notion. Customers may buy a car because they need transportation, but they will also buy it because it is fashionable, fuel-efficient or delivered ahead of the competition. All of these features represent value in the customer's mind.
Positioning	Positioning involves relating perceived value to the external environment. Generally, value is not an absolute; it is established as a perception on the part of the customer in relationship to something else, such as a competitor's offerings. In positioning a product, marketers select the values they want to emphasize for their products against those to be compared and the market (type of customers) they want to address. For example, a Mercedes car is positioned in promotion and price as a prestige car that provides an outward indication of power, wealth and prestige.
Promotion	Promotion encompasses the entire field of communication that results in consumer awareness about the product or service and the way it creates value for customers. It covers advertising, personal selling, sales promotion, public relations and publicity.
Pricing	Price represents what the customer must give up to receive the product. The price covers not only the product but also intangibles such as convenience, timeliness of delivery, ease of use or even how pleasurable it is to acquire the product. For successful transactions, customers must perceive that they are getting value for money.

Distribution	Distribution is the process of making sure that the product or service is available when and where it is wanted. It covers areas such as transportation, distribution channels and inventory practices. This involves both the intermediaries who carry out these various activities as well as the logistics of transporting and distributing the goods.
Relationship	A sale represents the establishment of a relationship between the seller and the buyer. If that relationship is to continue, the seller must demonstrate commitment and interest. At a minimum, the seller must be ready to provide whatever after-sales service may be required to keep the buyer satisfied.
Feedback	No marketing process can succeed without some form of feedback between customer and seller. Successful companies make sure to monitor how customers receive their products and services, and to establish mechanisms for adjusting products services or processes in response to customer concerns.

1.4 Key marketing concepts

Beyond the elements of marketing and sources of value and innovation, a number of key concepts govern the practice of marketing.

- **Differentiation** – demonstrating that a product or service is distinctively different is the essence of competition. Success goes to those who are creative in the ways they differentiate their products and services.

- **Creativity** – it is important to consider all of the ways by which your product or service can best appeal to your customers. This includes a whole range of factors, from tangible issues such as price, weight, efficiency and durability, to intangible ones such as prestige, life style issues or ensuring a comfortable personal chemistry between the sales person and the client. Factors such as service and quality are central to even the most durable and concrete products.

- **Market segmentation** – not all of a company's customers care about the same things or value features in the same way. The successful marketer will recognize these differences and develop strategies to address market segments in highly specific ways.

- **Relationships as assets** – especially today as more of the world's work is done through long-term contacts or via supplier-customer links that stretch out over many years, relationships with customers are a firm's most important asset. Like other assets, they need to be managed. After-sales service and maintenance packages have become an integral part of the sale for products such as automobiles. And ongoing upgrades at reduced costs are typical of the computer software industry.

- **Associations** – one of the most effective ways of positioning a product is to associate it with something that is already familiar to the customer. One of the most common forms of association involves product endorsements by high-profile personalities. There is a well-known Japanese TV ad (which you will not see in North America) showing a famous North American film star, now a politician, drinking a particular brand of beer after a harrowing ride on the subway. It worked for Japan, but is banned by the actor in North America. Associations also can be far subtler. For example, the names of deodorant soaps such as "Irish Spring" and "Coast" are associated with freshness, a major selling feature.

- **Partnerships and alliances** – marketers can strengthen their efforts through the synergies arising from partnerships and alliances. Walt Disney studios and McDonald's are among the most successful marketing organizations of all time. Their power and reach has been strengthened considerably through an ongoing alliance that offers toys based on Disney movies as part of McDonald's "Happy Meals." Children seeing the movie will want to visit the restaurant to get the toy. Children at the restaurant getting a "free toy" with their meal will be reminded of the movie and urge their parents to see it.

  Most of the North American fast-food franchises in Japan have joint venture partners. The partners are valuable for many reasons. One of the most important reasons is that most of the partners have real estate subsidiaries and these offices can select the best locations for walk-in foot traffic. There are some fast-food drive-in facilities in Japan (and Korea, Taiwan, Hong Kong, China, etc.) but walk-in traffic is the most important reason for success in high-density populations.

- **The importance of planning** – no enterprise can market successfully by mere instinct or accident, it depends on clear objectives, comprehensive research and careful implementation for success. The larger the business, the more likely it needs a written plan that can be clearly communicated and frequently reviewed.

1.5 Marketing functions

The most important function of a company's marketing department is to act as a link between customers and the company's other activities. The manager in charge of the marketing effort should be able to commit the company to the delivery of products or services required by customers, and other departments of the firm should honour that commitment. Clearly, close coordination is required to ensure that this really happens. The organizational structure needed to sustain this communication will depend on the size of the firm, its products and the scope of its operations.

The following are some other factors that influence how marketing functions will be organized:

- the stage of the firm's evolution (e.g. start-up, local focus, international orientation);

- the company's business (e.g. product, customer type, sources of value);

- environmental factors (e.g. market trends, competition);

- method of selling (e.g. direct or indirect); and

- ownership structure (e.g. is the company independent or is it a subsidiary?).

Planning

One of the most important elements in any successful marketing effort is the ability to plan. Planning involves both short- and long-term considerations. In the case of international trade, it must incorporate both a domestic and an international perspective. It should also deal with the aspects of customer acquisition, satisfaction and retention.

Short-term planning involves establishing marketing targets for a particular time period (e.g. for the coming year) and then providing for the kind of day-to-day operations needed to meet those targets. The short-term plan is, of necessity, part of the company's longer-term strategic plan.

Unlike the strategic plan, the short-term plan may be subject to periodic and even frequent revisions to keep up with changing circumstances. Separate short-term plans should be developed for each particular market in which a company hopes to be active. Line staff operating close to where the company interacts with its customers usually produces short-term plans.

Long-term planning involves not only a longer time horizon but also a strategic view of the entire company. More than just an aggregate of individual short-term plans, the long-term marketing plan goes beyond the results that might be derived from any one market: it presents a global view of the firm's overall direction, objectives and expectations.

Long-term plans are usually prepared by, or with, the direct involvement of the company's senior management.

Order processing and customer service

A key set of marketing functions involves order processing and customer service. Any company seriously interested in marketing abroad will have to provide facilities for responding to inquiries from potential foreign customers. Such inquiries may be concerned with product descriptions and technical specifications. More often, they involve the preparation of quotations specifying prices and conditions of delivery. Alternatively, clients may submit offers to which the company should respond promptly either with acceptance or with a counter-offer.

The order-processing function does not stop there. If both parties agree to a transaction, the order-processing department must ensure that the order is filled. This may involve communicating with the production department to schedule an additional run. Alternatively, it may require dealing with warehousing to transfer items out of inventory for shipment.

Finally, order processing will also involve taking measures to secure payment from the buyer. In the case of international trade, this can be a complex function involving the issuance of letters of credit or bills of exchange. The order-processing department will have to ensure that the appropriate documentation is prepared to support the transaction.

Sales

Sales are one of the functions normally associated with marketing. The way that a company organizes its sales efforts will depend on the nature of the product and the target market. For example, commodity items may be best handled through brokers and intermediaries. Even items destined for a mass consumer market might be handled most efficiently through a network of distributors. Such an approach saves the company the expense of investing in a marketing infrastructure of its own.

As products increase in terms of added value, exclusivity or price, the company may prefer to use more personal forms of selling. This may include the use of sales agents. In the case of international sales, the agent may originate from and should be familiar with the target market. This is a good strategy for marketing that involves a considerable degree of cultural awareness.

Alternatively, staff from the parent organization in Canada may be sent abroad to direct the sales effort. This is often the case where marketing the product requires specialized technical knowledge that may not be available locally. In the case of very large strategic transactions (e.g. entering into a multi-year exclusive agreement with a foreign distributor), the actual selling may be done on a one-to-one basis between the exporting firm's senior management and the key decision makers in the distribution organization.

However sales are organized and conducted, selling is an activity that requires both skill and sensitivity. Companies establishing an international sales group should pay close attention to training issues. Companies that already have an international sales force should use training to make sure that the skills of their representatives remain fresh and responsive to customers.

Promotion

Promotional activities (advertising, events management, dissemination of information) are another function typically associated with marketing. The key points to remember in organizing this function are to ensure that the promotional techniques:

- are appropriate to the product being sold (e.g. informational seminars may be appropriate for complex and leading-edge high-tech devices, while mass advertising is more effective for consumer goods);

- are appropriate to the target market (e.g. print advertising clearly will not work in a consumer market in which there is a large proportion of people who cannot, or do not, read); and

- reflect the inputs received from the sales organization (e.g. successful firms listen to what their customers want and do not try to force their own messages on a target market).

Chapter 4 of Team Canada Inc's Step-by-Step Guide to Exporting, found at **www.exportsource.ca**, proposes the following checklist of marketing materials.

Figure 3: Marketing tools and materials

Marketing Tool	Desired Impression	Are Yours...?
Business cards	Quality and excellence	<ul><li>easy to read</li><li>in appropriate language(s) (bilingual)</li><li>consistent throughout the organization</li><li>distinctive</li><li>informative</li><li>complete with address including area codes, country, cell phone, email, web site, and overseas branch office information</li><li>company logo</li></ul>
Brochures	World class	<ul><li>highlighting your uniqueness</li><li>easy to scan</li><li>download copy on the web page</li><li>informative</li><li>offset/laser printed</li><li>graphically pleasing</li></ul>
Customer testimonials	Company is highly recommended	<ul><li>representative</li><li>from top executives</li><li>included in brochure</li></ul>
Media pieces	Company is a recognized leader	<ul><li>quoted in brochure</li><li>reproduced on letterhead</li><li>displayed in office</li><li>mailed out</li></ul>
Videos/DVDs	Sophisticated	<ul><li>video in various formats or DVD</li><li>multilingual</li><li>professionally produced</li><li>feature and benefit oriented</li><li>short</li><li>easy to get</li></ul>

Marketing Tool	Desired Impression	Are Yours...?
Web site	Leading edge	<ul><li>professional looking</li><li>informative</li><li>judicious use of graphics</li><li>short company video, multilingual</li><li>updated regularly</li><li>email response option</li><li>online purchase option if appropriate</li><li>world-wide branch information</li></ul>

Distribution

A company's efficiency in getting its products to customers will go a long way toward determining the firm's image in the target market. However, it is very important to distinguish between the logistical and the marketing aspects of distribution. As a logistical function, distribution involves the mechanics and issues related to taking a product from the producers to the consumers. As a marketing concept, distribution pertains to the channels used to reach customers and embodies the notion of place in the marketing mix. The distribution channel is the logical place where the product should (must) be sold. Place (distribution) is driven by the target market and the positioning defined in the marketing strategy. For example, a small company producing expensive, high-quality children's clothing should not sell to Wal-Mart. It should go to small, specialized stores. To take another example, a firm cannot launch sophisticated sport equipment, targeting hi-end and professional users, and then distribute (place it) through Canadian Tire.

Moreover, certain customers may have special requirements regarding timing, packing, safety, or routing. This becomes absolutely critical in the case of international trade, where packaging and labelling requirements can differ widely from those in the Canadian domestic market. Two issues, in particular, need to be addressed.

One, the government in the target market may have quite specific regulations governing how products are to be packaged and how they are to be labelled. This may include permissible number of units per package (singly, in pairs, tens, dozens, etc.) as well as what materials can be used in the package. It may also specify what information must be contained on the label as well as the languages to be used.

Two, local cultural sensitivities may also have an influence on how products are packaged and labelled. For example, green is a colour associated with the Prophet Mohammed in Islamic countries and white is the colour of mourning in China. In some societies, the picture on a label signifies the contents of the package, so a picture of a smiling baby on a jar of baby food will definitely be misunderstood. Label designers might have to take this into account when designing packaging for such markets.

Information about such special requirements should be assembled during the course of initial market research. However, if that research has been less than thorough, it may reach the company after the fact, through the sales staff or the order-processing department. Regardless of how it is received, the group in charge of distribution will have to satisfy the requirement.

After-sales service

The ability to offer comprehensive, convincing and high quality after-sales service may be a key element in the marketing of a company's products. In many cases, such service is what distinguishes a product from either a commodity or the offerings of competitors.

Here, too, the company must understand customer requirements, ensure that human resources are available, and integrate its operations with the rest of the organization to ensure that information flows to where it is needed. In the case of international markets, however, after-sales service can represent quite a significant challenge.

1.6 Highlights

- Marketing is a process for identifying, anticipating and satisfying customer requirements profitably.

- Marketing is also putting together the right "marketing mix" of product, price, place and promotion.

- Marketing encompasses the functions of planning, order processing and customer service, sales, promotion, distribution and after-sales service.

Case questions for discussion

The following questions refer to the case that can be found in Appendix 1 at the end of this guide. Each chapter in this workbook concludes with questions about the case based on the contents of the chapter.

1. Which of the key principles discussed in this chapter has Mondetta followed in its approach?

2. How about your company?

2. Going Abroad: The Characteristics of International Marketing

Objectives

The objectives for this chapter are as follows:

- **Identify key international marketing challenges and explain how they differ from those of domestic marketing.**

- **State the key business considerations when developing international business projects.**

2.1 Deciding to go abroad

International marketing is exciting, challenging, and potentially profitable, but it costs more than domestic marketing – usually a lot more. In many cases, Canadian companies start on the road to international marketing when they receive an unsolicited order from outside the country. Alternatively, once they are well established domestically, they may look to international trade as a way of increasing their profits. Tapping into external markets can be achieved by both exporting and importing products or services. International trade covers a broad range of activities, including international marketing, finance, production and management.

International business influences all business in Canada – even very small companies that seem to have an exclusively domestic focus. Although they are affected by the activities of foreign entities doing business in this country, small domestic companies still focus on the local market: they are not operating internationally.

Technological development is behind much of the change observable in the world. Developments in telecommunications, computer applications and improved methods of shipping affect all Canadian companies. Companies at the cutting edge of technological innovation can find rich opportunities in the international arena. Rapid change also means, however, that the windows for each of these opportunities are ever narrower. A company's ability to track, anticipate and adapt to changes in the international marketplace determines its level of success.

However, no matter what kind of Canadian company is involved, international marketing is different. An international trade consultant was working for a domestically-oriented vice president who was attempting to enter the Japanese market. The consultant tried to explain that the Japanese way of doing business was different. "No problem" said the V.P., "You just tell them what I say, but you say it in Japanese." Companies that are successful domestically often do not understand that they cannot continue to do business in the same way when they go abroad.

2.2 International marketing is different!

Although the principles of marketing remain the same, international marketing differs from domestic marketing. There are several reasons why this is the case:

- Getting and staying close to the customer is more difficult at long range.

- Understanding customers from a different cultural environment with different cultural values is more difficult.

- Surveying and understanding customers may be difficult or even impossible in a foreign market using normal methods.

- Modifying or redesigning products to conform to foreign tastes and preferences may be difficult and costly.

- Being perceived as foreign is an added barrier that companies must overcome when marketing abroad.

- Communicating (e.g. advertising, media, sales techniques) may be quite different or less effective in the target market.

- Distributing goods over long distances poses an additional set of logistical challenges.

- Providing certain features may simply not be cost-effective at long distance.

- Providing after-sales service may be more difficult.

- Monitoring customer satisfaction may be impossible or the techniques for doing so may be different.

None of this means that it is not possible to do effective international marketing. What it does mean is that international marketing is more complex than domestic marketing. It requires commitment, resources and, above all, a different kind of market research.

Going beyond the research required for domestic marketing, the international marketer must also develop an understanding and appreciation of the following:

- differences in industrial, economic and technological levels between countries (e.g. varying standards, expectations, capabilities, skills);

- cultural differences (e.g. languages, values, aesthetics);

- political and legal differences;

- different business practices; and

- varying levels of competitive intensity.

The key is to adapt a good general idea to the needs and preferences of specific foreign audiences. Few international marketing plans will be successful unless local people shape them to reflect local realities and sensitivities. That is why companies seek the advice and counsel of advertising, marketing and communications professionals when attempting to penetrate foreign markets.

2.3 What to keep in mind

The following is a list of details companies should keep in mind when creating an international marketing organization. They are based on feedback from a number of experienced business people who have travelled and worked abroad as marketers.

Planning

- Define international marketing objectives (e.g. market share vs. profit).

- Have a clear picture of the company's international goals and objectives. A map of the short- and long-term business and marketing plans is needed.

- Select a market or geographic niche in which customer awareness does not have to be developed.

- Verify or have knowledge of international law. This is critical.

- Allow extra time. International marketing usually takes longer than estimated.

- Develop and test a good business case. Be pragmatic; do not "go international" just because it is in vogue.

- Develop a knowledge of counter-trade (barter) and draw up contingency plans if you cannot accommodate it as part of your trading.

- Do not create weaknesses at home by overextending yourself in foreign markets.

Commit to the long term: do not just fill in time while domestic sales are slow. Nothing makes distributors and customers more suspicious than an exporter who is in and out of the market.

Culture

- Develop cultural sensitivity. It will help you even in your home market.

- Conduct detailed research into the local culture. Cultural knowledge is a key to success.

- Make use of Canadian employees/consultants both in Canada and resident in the foreign market, who are experienced in the target market and speak the language. However, hire professional translators and interpreters (two different skill sets) for important business negotiations.

- Also hire and use local people where possible. It will eliminate many potential cultural misunderstandings in the long run.

- Insist that company representatives know at least some basics of the language of the target market. It may not be realistic for company executives to become fluent but at a minimum, senior firm representatives should learn a few basic phrases, know how to address people, and understand the types of salutations used in letters and other forms of communication.

- Engage qualified translators and interpreters able to translate or interpret in both languages. Such translators and/or interpreters may have to be available in Canada and in the target market. Initially, when a company is testing a foreign market, it may be content with external suppliers of the foreign language capability. As its commitment to the market grows, it may want to bring that capability in-house.

Knowledge of the foreign environment

- Actively seek and maintain overseas markets using continuous marketing research that captures the dynamic nature of international trade.

- Attend trade shows for market research and product development.

- Make use of Canada's leadership in the field of information technology. It helps in marketing research and in communications.

- Know your competition. Such knowledge can be illusory, since non-traditional products, as well as firms, may be competing against your product.

- Visit the marketplace and have face-to-face meetings with your potential customers – this is essential to success!

- Visit your customers regularly. Business outside of North America is described as "interpersonal relationships with money attached."

- Think of the world as one market, but with a variety of different cultures.

- Do not underestimate the business acumen of your customers (a temptation of owner-run businesses seeking to work in developing countries).

Financial considerations

- Make sure you have enough time, money and patience. International trading requires all three.

- Know about Canadian government export facilitator mechanisms (e.g. Team Canada Inc (TCI), International Trade Canada (ITCan), Export Development Canada (EDC), Canadian International Development Agency (CIDA)). This will help ease the difficulties encountered in trading.

- Understand the financial environment (e.g. exchange rates, restrictions, terms and methods of payment, especially letters of credit). Remember, a sale is not a sale until the account is credited.

- Understand the international system of "commissions." They are key in some countries. What others consider commissions, Canadians may consider "bribery".

- Research transportation alternatives. It can save your company money.

Networking and promotion

- Publicize your successes and invest in quality print materials to advertise the product or the company.

- Access international networking (marketing contacts) and distribution channels when you are a novice exporter.

Obtaining assistance

- Foster contacts with regional development banks, such as the Inter-American Development Bank in Washington or the Asian Development Bank (ADB) in Manila; such contacts can lead to opportunities.

- Know when not to go it alone: often, the best approach is to choose a partner to penetrate foreign markets.

- Have patience, but know when to call it quits. Many companies spent a lot of marketing dollars waiting for "the big sale" in the People's Republic of China.

Maintaining quality

- Ensure product quality. Avoid making errors or shipping poor quality products that are much more costly to repair or service abroad than in the domestic market.

- Provide customer service. It is more important than at home. A presence is needed in the foreign market.

2.4 Highlights

- **Although the principles of marketing remain the same, international marketing differs from domestic marketing.**

- **When companies increase their commitment to international markets, they must take into consideration certain factors such as planning, culture, knowledge of the foreign environment and so on.**

Case questions for discussion

1. Is Mondetta's international marketing approach different from their domestic approach? Explain how.

2. What differences will your company face in international markets?

3. The International Marketing Plan

Objectives

The objectives for this chapter are as follows:

- **Explain the role the international marketing plan plays in preparing international projects.**

- **Identify the essential marketing plan elements and propose how to assemble these into an effective plan.**

- **Discuss the issues to consider in successfully implementing an international marketing plan.**

3.1 The importance of planning

The international marketing plan is a component of the business plan. Regardless of its size, every business should have some kind of a plan that outlines its current position in the marketplace, strategic directions, expectations and objectives. Such plans are useful in getting a consensus within senior management. They can help employees understand how they can best contribute to a company's success. They can inform partners and investors about where a company is headed. In addition, banks and other lenders usually require them, along with a company balance sheet, income statement, cash flow projections, or a statement of changes in financial position, before they provide financing.

Plans are not meant to be treated rigidly. After the introduction and the executive summary, there should be a section on conclusions and recommendations. These should be concrete and based on current market conditions. However in the following sections, which detail the action plan, flexibility should be built in to meet changes in the marketplace. The plan should also specify how the company will adjust its plans if conclusions and proposed recommendations change.

A business plan need not be a single document. In many cases, it may be comprised of several linked but distinct subsections. A company may develop sub-plans dealing with technology, financing, logistics, human resources and marketing as part of an overall business plan. Each of these sub-plans would contribute to the goals and objectives set out in the broader plan, although how that contribution is made might be subject to independent adjustment.

A company called Pacific Business Marketing has a free business plan report called, How to develop and use a business plan. It is worth a look at the following:

www.business-marketing.com/html/marketplan.html

3.2 Why prepare an international marketing plan?

A company's international marketing plan is a key component of the business plan, because marketing is the way companies achieve their ultimate goal of profit. The international marketing plan serves as the foundation of the firm's overall international commercial strategy.

The purpose of the international marketing plan is to:

- provide a "road map" of who does what and when;

- understand the dynamics of each different foreign market;

- develop a profile of foreign customers;

- understand the tastes and preferences of foreign customers;

- evaluate the ability of the company's products and services to satisfy those customers;

- recommend product, service or process modifications required to better satisfy customers;

- develop promotional messages and sales techniques suited to the target market;

- devise distribution methods appropriate to the market;

- provide for after-sales service where necessary or desirable; and

- establish ways of monitoring, tracking and responding to customer reaction.

Companies that fail to prepare detailed marketing plans leave themselves vulnerable to unnecessary dangers. They run the risk of making mistakes, such as not identifying customers properly, sending them the wrong messages or shipping them the wrong product. A proper plan ensures that the company's actions are based on an understanding of the real situation of the target market, and not on wishful thinking. An international marketing plan will guide the firm through and deal with the hundreds of issues involved in penetrating complex and highly-competitive international environments.

It will help to:

- set out competitive advantages;

- forecast expected returns;

- detail probable costs;

- outline likely trade-offs;

- set priorities;

- specify marketing techniques suitable to the target market;

- suggest the systems (e.g. communications, logistics) required to serve the market; and

- develop an action plan.

Although a plan may help to forecast expected returns from a market, it is more than just an exercise in sales forecasting. In planning, it is important to grasp the difference between strategic and tactical marketing plans.

A **strategic plan** addresses broad issues of corporate direction and positioning:

- Which markets should the company be in?

- What market share is it looking for?

- What does it expect to achieve?

A **tactical plan** focuses on short-term implementation issues:

- What marketing techniques should be used in the next campaign?

- Who will implement them?

- What immediate results are expected?

A strategic plan is not just the sum of a series of tactical plans:

> *Most managers prefer to sell the products they find easiest to sell to those customers who offer the least line of resistance. By developing short-term, tactical marketing plans first and then extrapolating them, managers merely succeed in extrapolating their own shortcomings. It is a bit like steering from the wake – all right in calm, clear waters, but not so sensible in busy and choppy waters! Preoccupation with preparing a detailed one -year plan first is typical of those many companies, which confuse sales forecasting and budgeting with strategic marketing planning...[4]*

The strategic marketing plan should be developed before any detailed sales forecasts. Finally, it should be emphasized that a company needs a separate section for each market targeted. Each foreign market is unique. It has specific characteristics that demand specific responses from the company. There is no such thing as the single best approach to international marketing. Each market and each company addressing that market will require a customized and a distinctive strategy.

3.3   The elements of an international marketing plan

The international marketing plan is a written summary of the firm's export goals in a specific overseas market, the strategy to be followed, the organization of the resources needed to meet that strategy, and a feedback and reporting mechanism to measure progress. A clear and concise marketing plan is an essential element of a service firm's export strategy. In fact, the organization

---

[4]   Malcolm H.B. McDonald. *Marketing Plans: How to Prepare Them, How to Use Them with Disk.* 4th ed. (Oxford: Butterworth-Heinemann, 1999).

may choose to develop a series of marketing plans based on different lines of business and different markets.

There are many sources of information about what goes into an international marketing plan. Useful tools and links to other sites offering information, templates and other utilities can be accessed through ExportSource. The Step-by-Step Guide to Exporting found on the site, also contains a guide to developing an international marketing plan.

www.exportsource.ca/stepbystep

Sample marketing plan outline

The following simple one-page guideline can be used to develop a basic international marketing plan. Sources of information should be included to make it easy to validate and update information as circumstances change.

1. Executive summary

State the purpose of the marketing plan, indicating an overview of the objectives, and how the marketing plan will be used to make a positive contribution to the firm's exporting activities.

2. Analysis of the product or service

Describe the business, its history, size and resources. Describe the product or service offering, its unique selling points and how marketable these offerings might be in an international setting. Provide the key reasons for exporting. Demonstrate that the firm's core competency and competitive advantage is world class.

3. Analysis of the target market

Describe the target market including size and trends. Include an analysis of key economic, social, political and cultural considerations. Specify the sector in which the company hopes to operate and provide detail of sector size, segments, growth trends and driving forces in that industry. Provide a detailed profile of your target customer, needs, buying patterns, expectations regarding price, quality and service, as well as factors influencing purchasing decisions.

4. Competitive analysis

Perform a detailed competitive analysis. It will help you to plan the positioning of your product or service offerings, and to make pricing and marketing decisions. Who are the main competitors? Evaluate the strengths and weaknesses of major competitors. Outline the company's competitive advantage vis-à-vis competitors.

5. Goals and targets

State the firm's objectives in terms of market share, revenue and profit expectations. Indicate what position the company would like to occupy in the target market. Explain how it will go about achieving this position.

6. Entry strategy

Given political characteristics, business environment, regulatory considerations and any other significant factors, what is the preferred strategy for entering in that market: direct export? indirect export through agents or distributors? local partnerships? methods of sale and distribution recommended?

7. Marketing strategy

The marketing strategy sets out details about how the company intends to achieve its overall strategic objectives. It includes information about issues such as:

- What products or services does the company plan to market?

- What sets the company apart from the competition? Why are they unique?

- How will it price its products and services? Do trade terms affect the cost?

- Does the price compare with the competition? If it is higher, why? If it is lower, what are the reasons?

- Where will the company market its products or services?

- Which segment of the market will the company focus on?

- Is the target segment large enough to make the business worthwhile?

- Does the company's marketing material reflect the professionalism of the firm?

- Should it budget for media advertising and a public relations campaign?

- Where are the potential clients? How will the firm reach them?

- What are the fundamental elements linking the company's clients?

8. Implementation plan

List in detail the specific activities required to implement the marketing plan indicating target dates and who will perform the activities. Include a description of the human resources required as well as their capabilities. Prepare a detailed marketing budget based on the implementation plan.

9. Evaluation plan

Design a plan that will allow for the evaluation of the marketing plan at various intervals to determine if the goals are being achieved and what if any modifications may be required.

10. Conclusion

Include a half-page conclusion that shows how the overall marketing plan fits into the company's overall business plan. A PowerPoint presentation could be prepared, covering the main points in the plan. This presentation could be used as part of an elevator pitch to sell the international marketing plan.

3.4   Implementing the international marketing plan

The last but very important part of the marketing plan is working out an action plan for implementation. What contacts does the company already have in the target market? What types of professional assistance or partners might be useful? Should the company seek to develop a relationship with in-country professionals such as lawyers or tax advisors, joint venture partners, investors or R&D partners? Are there potential partners in Canada who can assist with the venture?

Once a strategy has been prepared, the company must designate a champion to assume responsibility for implementing the plan. That individual should be provided with concrete milestones and specific targets, as well as adequate resources in terms of staff, training, control and compensation.

The following factors need to be considered:

- Given that "going international" can be costly in the short term; does the firm have the financial strength and cash flow to fund the international marketing exercise? For example, mounting a sales force in a foreign country is a drain on cash flow given that foreign receivables generally take longer to collect.

- Does the firm have the specialized skills needed to conduct international trade? Does staff have to be trained or new staff hired to make the required skills available to the organization? Specialized skills include knowledge of local culture, language, international pricing and distribution channels.

Meeting the challenge of export and competition is everybody's business and should not be relegated to a small segment of the staff. In terms of international trade training, this means that human resource development is needed at many different levels in the organization. An export-focused human resource development program should address the following performance issues: recruitment, induction, development, motivation, empowerment, evaluation, recognition, reward and retention.

Ideally, a strong, well-qualified and well-funded international marketing and sales organization should be in place for successful selling abroad. This involves not only time and financial resources but also the commitment of senior management. If top-level management is not committed to (i.e. willing to participate directly) the marketing aspect of exporting, the company should seek alternative avenues, such as the use of an export-trading house. Moreover, if adequate funding is not available, as is often the case in companies striving to remain "lean," some attention will have to be devoted to investigating and developing alternative sources of financing. If internal resources are not available, a foreign opportunity may have to be structured in such a way as to secure the support of a commercial lending institution or the interest of an investor.

Even the best thought-out plans may need to be modified to accommodate the dynamic nature of the international marketplace. The final step in the process of preparing a marketing plan is to develop a series of contingency plans in case things turn out differently. The management team should identify several possible alternative scenarios and have operational plans ready to meet any new set of circumstances.

Finally, it is important that the strategy be monitored regularly and progress fed back to the management of the company. The results should be measured against the export goals and objectives. Mechanisms should also be instituted to ensure that, when necessary, product, process and service adjustments can be made to improve performance.

3.5 Presenting the international marketing plan

In making a presentation of the marketing plan, keep the following points in mind:

- Open the discussion with a brief statement of the proposal. The length of this presentation depends on the size and complexity of the venture, but it is advisable to err on the side of excessive brevity and fill in additional details in response to questions.

- Keep focused on bottom-line priorities but remain open to exploring various types of responses and arrangements. All terms and conditions should be explored carefully before going forward.

- Don't attempt to hide or minimize the real risks involved in the venture. Any such attempt will only cause suspicion and lead to loss of credibility.

- End the meeting when scheduled. Extended meetings offer more opportunity for losing focus or betraying weaknesses.

- Note any objections or criticisms that are made. In some cases, such comments can be used to revise the original proposal, either for the same group, or for another prospect. In others, such criticisms may point to a fundamental weakness in the project that might require a rethinking of the strategy.

- Always offer to supply additional information should it be required. If a request is received, respond as quickly as possible.

3.6 Highlights

- **A plan outlines your strategic directions, expectations and objectives.**

- **Companies need a solid and credible international marketing plan if they are to succeed in export markets.**

- **Once a strategy has been prepared, an individual must take responsibility for the implementation of the plan.**

Case questions for discussion

1. What information from the articles would lead us to conclude that Mondetta has an international marketing plan?

2. Does your company have an international marketing plan? If not, when are you going to develop one?

4. The Market Entry Strategy

Objectives

The objectives for this chapter are as follows:

- **Explain how to design a focused international marketing strategy for a company.**

- **Identify the appropriate exporting method for a company from the different options available.**

4.1 A note on Incoterms

Before proceeding with this chapter, make sure you are familiar with Incoterms 2000, the most recent version. (The International Chamber of Commerce in Paris updates Incoterms every 10 years). It is never too early to learn these terms since a knowledge of Incoterms is knowledge of the export process.

See Appendix 6, a chart summarizing the most commonly used Incoterms, and Appendix 7, an illustration showing how Incoterms apply to the various stages of the export process. Pay close attention to EXW and CIF in particular. An EXWorks price is calculated on the basis of selling at the exporting firm's warehouse. A CIF (cost, insurance, freight) price is calculated on the basis of delivering goods to a port in the buyer's market. Several different sources have been given. Each presents Incoterms in a different way.

www.mapsupport.com/thedatabase/impex/incoterm

www.pbb.com/incoterms/incoterms2000.pdf

www.exportinsurance.com/incoterms.htm

www.cbsc.org/alberta/tblcfm?fn=incoterm

4.2 Selecting a strategy

Many different factors should be considered when deciding how to enter a foreign market. Direct exporting of a finished product is common, but it is only one of several strategies that Canadian firms use when going global. For example, high transportation costs or high tariffs could mean that a firm's product cannot be competitive in a foreign market if it enters using a conventional route. Other alternatives may be available, however. Firms should explore a wide variety of strategies for selling to customers outside Canada. For information on market-entry strategies, go to *Take a World View: Export Your Services.*

www.exportsource.ca/worldview

Apart from conventional shipping of end products, alternative strategies include licensing designs or technology, franchising a marketing process, investing in a foreign branch plant or setting up a manufacturing joint venture in collaboration with a local firm in the foreign market.

Exporters also vary their strategy from country to country and from regional market to regional market. For example, a firm might easily be able to sell its product in the United States, but find that transportation and the costs of product adaptation make it difficult to export profitably to Southeast Asia. That does not mean giving up on the Southeast Asian market. Instead of trying to transport its products to Southeast Asia, the firm might choose to set up a wholly-owned foreign branch plant in the region – or perhaps find a joint venture partner there to assemble or manufacture the product locally.

Firms need to tailor their entry to ensure that their products are as competitively positioned as possible. Export strategies may also have to be modified as conditions change.

Issues such as tariff and non-tariff barriers, the cost of customizing the product to meet local market requirements, currency fluctuations and transportation costs will all affect the final decision. While adapting to the market of the host country could significantly increase costs, the resulting increase in sales volume may make it well worthwhile.

4.3 Niche marketing

One key strategic consideration is to choose what size and breadth of market a company can reasonably accommodate. Because most Canadian companies do not have the critical mass and financial resources to penetrate foreign markets across a broad front, it is also important to understand the advantages of niche marketing as it applies to specific market-entry strategies.

Niche marketing involves specialization in narrowly-focused product or service areas. This strategy is particularly appropriate for small- and medium-sized companies, which in many cases do not have the skills and resources to compete against large global companies that cover wide market areas.

A company in Vancouver has concentrated on the export of packaged seafood products. They have a particular niche. Japanese tourists, and increasingly Canadian business people with important contacts in Japan, order their products in Vancouver and the product is delivered in Japan, by courier, from a company warehouse in Japan.

Canada has many "second-tier" international companies, which are big at home but small by world standards. These companies have a specialized product or expertise that they sell to the world market as niche players. Examples include: Royal Trust in personal banking, SHL Systemhouse in systems consulting, Cascades Inc. in paper products and Spar Aerospace in specialized space technologies.

4.4 Indirect exporting (through intermediaries)

Another important strategic consideration is how much of the export effort a company wants to take on when it goes global. Often international trade consultants will hear from a company about how much it is exporting and how the foreign market likes the product. When they ask how the firm ships its goods, they may hear something like: "We don't get involved in those details, we ship the stuff EXWorks, the foreign buyer picks it up at our warehouse, we get paid right away – none of that letter of credit stuff – and if the final customer has a problem, our buyer handles it."

Is this firm exporting? Its products are ending up in a foreign market, but it has no control over them after they leave the warehouse. It has made the sale, but has not gained control of the market.

Indirect exporting is good for many companies. Especially those who are used to the domestic market and don't have the knowledge, experience or the desire to get involved in international shipping, banking, and documentation. Sometimes, indirect exporting is the best (or the only) way for a company to export. There are advantages and disadvantages in both indirect and direct exporting. Which is better depends on the nature of the business and the size of the market, among other factors.

Indirect exporting is typified by the BC winegrower who was asked if he exported any of his wine to Japan. "Oh yes," he replied. "Some guy from Japan comes by once a year and buys a whole bunch. We have no idea where it goes."

A door manufacturer will sell doors to a prefab housing company who then exports the complete house. The doors get into the foreign market indirectly. At a later date, the door company may decide to get into the foreign market directly and develop its own distributors/customers in the market.

An indirect exporter sells to a Canadian-based trading company or some other organization in Canada, which then assumes responsibility for marketing and shipping abroad.

A company involved in indirect exporting usually does not have to worry about export documentation, foreign exchange or overseas marketing research since this is left to the intermediary. On the other hand, once a product is sold to an intermediary such as a trading company, the seller relinquishes control over the product, its pricing, promotion or further disposition.[5]

There are six basic approaches to indirect exporting. Firms can sell their goods to:

- Canadian-based trading houses,

- export management companies (EMCs),

- foreign government purchasers,

- representatives of foreign companies,

- Canadian federal agencies acting for foreign clients,

- Canadian manufacturers that export goods abroad.

---

[5] A good discussion on trading companies is in: FITTskills, *International Market Entry and Distribution: Participant's Manual*, (Ottawa: Forum for International Trade Training, revised 2002), pp.110-114.

A company that has never exported and receives a foreign order from a Canadian-based buyer is probably better off exporting indirectly. However if that firm wants to become involved in exporting directly to foreign markets, then the company had better prepare itself by mastering the complexities of the exporting process.

The next figure compares three different types of export intermediaries. Companies that export indirectly would deal with such intermediaries in Canada, relying on them to take their exports into foreign markets. Companies that export directly could find themselves dealing with the same types of intermediaries but based in their target markets abroad. In such cases, the exporting company would assume responsibility for the export process up to the point that the export is delivered into the hands of foreign customers or intermediaries.

Figure 4: Common export methods

Export trading house	Agent	Distributor
Can either enter into a contractual agreement with the exporter or purchase goods from the exporter	Enters into contractual agreements on behalf of the exporter	Purchases the goods from the exporter
May carry inventory	Does not store the goods but may have a small inventory	Carries inventory
May take title to the goods for resale or may act as an agent for goods that remain the property of the exporter	Exporter retains title to the goods	Takes title to and control over the goods
Sets the retail price	Does not set the retail price	Sets the retail price
Assumes risks if it assumes title to the goods	Does not assume risk	Assumes risk once the goods are in hand
Collects payment for goods sold	Does not handle payment, but receives a commission from the exporter after the latter receives payment	Pays the exporter once the goods are delivered to the distributor
Trade name and trademark may be used depending on the type of arrangement between the exporter and the trading house	Trade name and trademark kept by the exporter	Use of trademark is often restricted; may repackage and sell goods under own trade name

Export trading house	Agent	Distributor
Organization can be a cooperative or affiliated type, specializing in single commodities such as grain, pulp and paper, fish and agri/food sectors	May handle several non-competing lines at the same time and usually wants exclusivity in marketing or territory	Generally carries a variety of product lines
Conducts own marketing and promotional activities	Does not control the marketing methods	Plans and carries out its own marketing efforts
May act either as an independent or as a contractor	May act either as an independent contractor or as an employee	Operates as an independent
Is self-financed	Is financed by the exporter	Is self-financed
Can provide after-sales service	Does not arrange service or warranty which are responsibilities of the exporter	Provides service and warranty
Is responsible for liability or local taxation in taking title to goods	Is not responsible for liability or local taxation	Assumes responsibility for liability and local taxes

4.5   Direct exporting

When Canadian companies export directly, they often sell to the same types of companies in the foreign market as they do when exporting indirectly. A firm is exporting directly any time it is selling to a client abroad and is being paid by that client. It is exporting directly even if it is selling to the client on an EXWorks, FAS or FOB basis.

The Canadian Wheat Board (**www.cwb.ca**) is a farmer-controlled organization that markets wheat and barley grown by western Canadian producers. The Board sells wheat on an Incoterms FOB basis. The wheat is loaded on board a ship. The customer, usually a foreign government, arranges the ship charter and marine insurance. This is a direct export.

Foreign trading houses can be customers. Selling EXW to a Japanese trading company in Canada means selling to a Canadian middleman, who will pay in Canada and then sell the goods in Japan or some other country. In that case, the firm is exporting indirectly.

There are, of course, independent agents in the foreign market. They will represent a firm on a commission basis. They do not take title to the goods, but they do help to make a sale to a customer in that market. That customer may be an end-user or it can be a distributor in that market.

Foreign distributors may buy directly from the exporter on a CIF basis, but that is not absolutely necessary. Even if a firm has an agent helping it in a market, the agent is representing the firm and is paid by it. Agents are especially useful in a foreign market where there are several large distributors, each specializing in a segment of the market.

When selling to a foreign buyer, a good practice is to quote the goods CIF (to the buyer's foreign port), make all the shipping arrangements, handle all the details of the irrevocable confirmed letter of credit, and finance the export: that is a direct export.

A customer can be anyone in the foreign market. It might be a foreign-based trading company or a distributor in that market. Increasingly, even end-users are importing into their own markets. For example, in Japan and Korea, homebuilders buy several container loads of building materials, lumber, plywood, or flooring.[6] Instead of purchasing through trading companies, small distributors are now bypassing the trading companies and buying directly from Canadian suppliers on a CIF basis.

Direct exporting allows the supplier control over both pricing and promotion. For new potential exporters, the most common and effective way to arrange for direct export is to go on trade missions where potential buyers of Canadian products can be met in person.

Another effective way of preparing to export directly is to make a private trip and prearrange appointments with potential buyers using the company's own contacts or the services of Canadian trade commissioners.

Selling directly to an end-user located in another country is appropriate when only the manufacturer's sales staff can provide the depth of knowledge or expertise essential to sell the products. It might also be appropriate if the firm is addressing a market of relatively few potential customers (e.g. managing a hydroelectric project for a foreign government) or where potential customers are concentrated in a relatively small geographical area.

Direct exporting is the most appropriate way of selling industrial products and it can be appropriate for quite different sectors. For example, it can be used to sell highly-priced and highly-technical products or services such as airplanes, ships, and hydroelectric turbines for generators or industrial machinery. Alternatively, it may be used to market a wide range of goods or services, as when a foreign retailer buys an entire line of products from a Canadian food processor.

Finally, in direct exporting, it is up to the exporter to ensure that the target country does not have restrictions on foreign direct sales and to determine the degree of preference that potential customers may have for local representation.

---

[6] See "Chip of Choice", *The Province* (Vancouver), March 28, 2004, p. A64

4.6 Highlights

- Companies can enter markets through direct exporting or indirect exporting. Both offer advantages and disadvantages.

- Increasingly, smaller-sized exporters are resorting to niche marketing techniques in order to focus more closely on the specific markets for which their products or services are tailored.

Case questions for discussion

1. In what situation should Mondetta consider direct marketing? Indirect marketing?

2. If Mondetta has an exclusive agent in Italy, and the Canadian subsidiary of an Italian company wants to buy from Mondetta on an EXWorks basis, what should Mondetta do?

3. What is Mondetta's niche? What did they do to develop this niche?

4. Has your firm developed a target niche? If not, what do you think the company should look for?

5. Cultural Differences and International Marketing

Objectives

The objectives for this chapter are as follows:

- **Explain how cultural factors apply to international marketing.**

- **Evaluate the impact of cultural differences in successfully marketing products abroad.**

- **Explain the intercultural differences to consider when using mass marketing techniques for a foreign population.**

5.1 The impact of culture on trade

A Japanese businessman in Vancouver had a low opinion of Canadian business people; especially lumber traders because he thought they were lazy. He liked to work quite late in the evening and would complain that the Canadians were never in the office after 4:30 pm. This was his time to call Tokyo as the offices were just opening up in Asia. The businessman normally started just after 9:00 am in the morning and eventually was surprised to learn that the Canadians were usually at work by 7:00 am or sooner as they had to call their customers and contacts in eastern North America where it was already 10:00 am in the morning.

Understanding cultural differences goes beyond intellectual appreciation. Marketers must develop "cultural sensitivity" to adjust their organization and operations so that they can make appropriate changes to their business practices and promotional programs. Companies need to have a structure or approach to evaluate culture itself, and must incorporate cultural influences into marketing plans or sales negotiations.

A Canadian trade consultant visiting China for the first time visited a Volkswagen showroom in Shanghai. The consultant could read basic Chinese and had a background in automotive manufacture, marketing and transportation. He was surprised to discover that there were only three cars in the showroom. The smaller one was obviously for consumers. There was a medium-sized one outfitted as a taxi. The third was marked with large characters for "Public Safety" written on the door and was outfitted as a police car. There were clearly three specialty markets in Shanghai.

5.2 The methods by which we communicate

Communication, sometimes defined as the exchange of meaning, can involve what is said, how it is said, what is left unsaid and what is conveyed by non-verbal means. In fact, a lot of meaning may be conveyed by non-verbal signals that are either consciously given or given without the sender being aware of it. In one study, it was revealed that only 7 percent of a message is communicated by words while 93 percent of the message is communicated through non-verbal means such as the tone of voice (how it is said) and facial expressions, hand gestures and posture.

Communication is dependent on and determined by the culture in which it occurs and communication practices will vary from culture to culture.

In marketing, one must build up sensitivity to language and the communication of information. The real challenge comes in communicating among cultures that have evolved different symbols, references and methods for conveying meaning. This is more than just a matter of language. It also requires sensitivity to national outlook and the nuances of meaning.

Different societies emphasize different values. In Spain or Greece, personal honour is paramount; in Switzerland, dependability is a core value. In East Asia, personal relationships are important, and they are essential in Latin America.

Written communication

When writing letters to overseas contacts or developing marketing materials for them, companies are well advised to write clearly, directly and simply. They should avoid humour, innuendoes or slang that might be misinterpreted. They should include polite and diplomatic sentiments if these are appropriate to the targeted culture (such as when writing to Japanese or Middle Eastern trading partners).

It is important, however, to know what is or is not appropriate in different cultures. Even seemingly straightforward information can be misleading. To avoid confusion, for example, numbers should be checked and units of weight or measurement clearly identified since they may be different in the trading partner's country. It is generally better to provide too much descriptive information about a product, packaging or shipping arrangements than not enough.

Where appropriate, companies should make an effort to provide written marketing materials in the first language of their potential trading partners. However, quality of the written materials is absolutely essential and scrimping on translation costs represents a potentially fatal false economy.

If a company cannot be assured of a first-rate translation, it would do better to send the materials in English or French. The seeming "discourtesy" of using one of these languages (acknowledged to be the languages of international business) is probably preferable to appearing ignorant or inarticulate in the foreign partner's own language.

Legal contracts will have to be drawn up in the language of the seller and that of the buyer. In this case, accurate translations are absolutely vital.

Non-verbal communication

Non-verbal communication, or the "silent language," is subtle, and usually spontaneous. It involves several dimensions:

- **Body language** (e.g. movement, gesture, posture, facial expression, gaze, touch, attentive listening and distancing) – in Greece or Italy, body language is an important part of interpersonal communication. In some other countries, such as in Denmark, people are less given to physical expression and most of the meaning in a conversation is conveyed in the words.

- **Object language** (e.g. signs, designs, artifacts, clothing, personal adornment) – some cultures, such as the Italian, put considerable emphasis on external appearance, especially clothing. And cultures interpret designs very differently. The bright red or yellow colours that are usual in a North American "power tie" are regarded as loud and tasteless by Spaniards. The Israelis often do not wear ties, and the same is true for the warmer parts of Australia.

- **Environmental language** (e.g. colour, lighting, architecture, space, direction, natural surroundings) – it is well known, for example, that colours have different connotations in other countries. White is associated with death in China, while green is considered sacred in Muslim countries because it is associated with the Prophet Mohammed.

The crucial area of non-verbal communication presents business people with some of their most challenging moments abroad.

5.3 Social considerations

International Trade Canada has a cultural web site (with links) for most of the countries of the world. This site provides basic information on the history, geography, culture, politics, economy and media of various countries:

www.e-thologies.com

Business does not exist in a vacuum nor can it be conducted without reference to the society in which it operates. Companies must be aware of, understand and be sensitive to social norms and how they will influence the way business is done in the target country. In particular, they should be aware of the following when designing their marketing strategy:

- religion, religious practices, holidays, forms of observance, what is sacred, and prohibitions;

- attitudes to societal factors (e.g. family, work, leisure, the country, the world outside);

- concepts of right and wrong, guilt, shame, ethical standards, values and responses related to personal characteristics (e.g. honour, generosity, integrity, decisiveness);

- personal greetings and introductions;

- entertaining business associates;

- the etiquette of gift giving;

- material culture (e.g. standards of living, spending priorities);

- aesthetics (e.g. approach to design, standards of beauty);

- personal space;

- role of family, friends and other relationships;

- attitudes toward achievement, authority, material possessions;

- friendship patterns;

- dietary taboos and restrictions; and

- mealtime patterns.

There is an interesting book, which covers social consideration in many different cultures:

Terri Morrison, Wayne A Conaway and George A. Borden *Kiss, bow, or shake hands: how to do business in sixty countries*. Holbrook Mass.: Adams Media Corporation, 1995.

Books on the same subject are available in the business section of the local or university library.

5.4   Business protocol

Business and social etiquette are important attributes to success in marketing overseas. Being aware of the different rules of intercultural etiquette will ensure rewarding personal and business relationships.

A useful web site on this topic is: **www.executiveplanet.com**.

In undertaking negotiations abroad:

- Use names and titles correctly.

- Be sensitive to the fact that businesswomen may be expected to greet their host or counterpart differently than men in certain cultures.

- Adapt to the greeting style of each country or region within a country.

- Learn the use, presentation, hidden meanings and importance of business cards. Make sure your name is written in a way your hosts can understand and pronounce. For example in Korea, make sure there is a *hangul* (Korean alphabet) equivalent of your name and in Japan that your name is also written in *katakana* (Japanese phonetics). When choosing a set of Chinese characters for your name, watch two things: make sure that the characters give a Mandarin pronunciation for your name and make sure that you have it checked with several Mandarin speakers. It is easy to unintentionally write a name with goofy connotations in Chinese.

- Find out what is appropriate attire for business and social settings.

- Be aware of conversational styles and avoid slang or jargon.

- Find out in advance about gestures or body language that may cause offence.

- Arrange the itinerary to avoid holidays, feast days and other special periods when businesses might be closed.

- Remain patient – time has different meanings in different cultures.

As a matter of general principle:

- Disagree agreeably; always remaining respectful and polite to the host even if there is no agreement.

- Learn how to say "thank you" in the host's way.

- Accept hospitality graciously.

- Be familiar with the normal hours of work: they may not correspond to what is typical in Canada.

- If invited to a home, learn the correct protocol for spouses, gifts and expressions of thanks.

- Master the entertaining style of the host country, including banquets and other business receptions.

- Know what time it is in the country being called when communicating by telephone or fax. Remain patient on the line, and make allowances for delays and echoes. With the advent of email, this consideration is less important. Email can be sent anytime.

- Appreciate that gift giving is a normal part of business worldwide, but remain sensitive to the possibility that gifts might be misinterpreted.

This last point raises a matter that can cause Canadian business people some difficulty abroad – the difference between gift giving and bribery. The practice of offering gifts as tokens of appreciation is common throughout the world. It is important to have some gifts that are representative of Canada, particularly in East Asia. In the past, a bottle of whiskey was considered appropriate, but in the 21st century more appropriate items are native art works, a glossy photo book on Canada or even some local delicacy. One visiting businessman gave gifts of specialty jams, which were appreciated by the host's family.

In some countries, what we would term bribery is not only a fact of life but also a prerequisite for getting something accomplished. In other countries, particularly in those trying to combat corruption, bribery is severely punished and even simple gift giving is discouraged, lest it be misunderstood. There are no easy rules for dealing with this issue.

The Canadian government has supported the 1997 OECD convention on the bribery of foreign public officials. The result was Bill S-21, The Corruption of Foreign Public Officials Act, which came into effect, February 14, 1999.

The act itself can be found by going to the following web site and then typing S-21 in search terms:

www.parl.gc.ca

The best advice for Canadian firms to follow is to investigate the specific conditions of the target market, talk to other Canadian companies already doing business there and then exercise common sense.

5.5 Tips for successful cross-cultural negotiations

A successful negotiation is one in which both parties gain. The art of cross-cultural negotiation can be a minefield or a gold mine, depending on the approach used. Successful international negotiators:

- are comfortable with the idea that they are the foreigners;

- are organized before and during the trip so that they are fresh and sharp at the destination;

- learn about the manners and customs of the people with whom they want to do business;

- adjust the pace and style of negotiating to that of their hosts;

- develop negotiating skills and leave nothing to chance or charm;

- learn when to say no and when to walk away from a deal that is not right;

- have enough authority to negotiate the deal without having to refer to headquarters;

- never get involved in discussions or comments about any country's politics, religion, way of life, business ethics or other potentially sensitive topics;

- always respect the terms of the contracts as they are negotiated and agreed upon;

- are very clear on the terms of the business agreements they enter into, whether formally or informally;

- understand and respect deadlines as defined in the host country.

In conducting negotiations abroad, the experienced international trader will never engage in a side conversation, in English or French, that is not meant for the others at a meeting, and never assume that such a conversation is in any way private and not understood by others. There is always a risk that someone will overhear and understand, which could be embarrassing.

5.6 Cultural sensitivities in mass marketing

A different set of challenges is presented when companies employ mass marketing to reach customers across an entire society. Marketing literature abounds with stories of marketing disasters that resulted from inadequate research into the language and culture of the target market.

One fundamental imperative is that companies seeking to enter a foreign market must verify the meaning and acceptability of their brand name, logo and slogans in the language of the country.

Above all, they must make sure that they do not have negative, offensive or inadvertently comic connotations. It is never safe to assume that an advertising campaign that worked in Canada will be equally effective in another culture.

Companies and people today are more aware of intercultural names. Some of these names, which may have been thought strange, or inappropriate, by an earlier generation in North America, are now quite acceptable. "Hello Kitty" is a popular motif in East Asia and North America. Pokemon has been a popular cartoon character for some time. There is a soft drink, popular in Japan and liked by Canadians who live there. The name "Pokari Sweat" probably would not sell at this moment in Canada, but might in the future. There is another more traditional summer drink made from fermented milk, again quite liked by Canadian residents in Japan. It is called Calpis, and because of its name, might be harder to sell in Canada.

The following are only a few of the better known marketing horror stories. Companies today seem to have learned from these examples:

A ball point pen made by Parker Pen was known everywhere as the *Jotter*- everywhere, that is, except in certain Latin American markets where the word meant a jockstrap. The company faced problems in Mexico when it designed a marketing campaign for ballpoint pens around the theme, "It won't leak in your pocket and embarrass you." Unfortunately, they used the wrong word and the ads actually said, "It won't leak in your pocket and get you pregnant".

When Coca-Cola was first introduced into China, it was rendered as *ke-kou-ke-la*, which meant "bite the wax tadpole" or "female horse stuffed with wax," depending on the dialect. Thousands of signs had already been printed when this was discovered. The company then researched 40,000 Chinese characters to come up with *ko-kou-ko-le*, which implies "happiness in the mouth".

The familiar slogan of "Pepsi Comes Alive" was translated into Chinese for the Taiwanese market, but came out as "Pepsi brings your ancestors back from the grave".

Kentucky Fried Chicken's slogan of "finger-lickin' good" was first translated into Chinese as "eat your fingers off".

Not all of the horror stories involve the clumsiness of North American firms trying to enter overseas markets. Foreign companies have shown themselves to be equally inept in marketing to English-speaking audiences.

The issue of cultural differences has received considerable attention in international marketing and it is important, but it should also be kept in proper perspective. Most foreign business people are also sensitive to cultural differences. They recognize that they live in a global economy and they will understand that you come from a different background.

As long as the deal is attractive to both sides, they are not likely to worry that you have not captured every nuance of local custom. In this sense, cultural appreciation can be useful in opening doors, breaking down barriers, creating a positive climate and facilitating discussions, but it is no substitute for the deal itself.

5.7 Highlights

- When a promising market is identified, you should find out as much as possible about the cultural characteristics of the market.

- Communicating efficiently is important. Less than 10 percent of a message is communicated by words and over 90 percent is communicated through non-verbal means.

- Marketing strategies must be designed in accordance with the local social considerations and business protocol.

Case questions for discussion

1. Can you identify the cultural differences that Mondetta has faced as they have entered each new market?

2. If they expand into other international markets, will they face other differences?

3. What cultural differences do you think your firm will face when they "go international"? Is your firm facing cultural differences now?

6. Political, Legal and Regulatory Considerations

Objectives

The objectives for this chapter are as follows:

- **Explain how political, legal and regulatory factors may apply to doing business abroad.**

- **Identify the political, legal and regulatory factors that can have an impact on an international marketing strategy.**

6.1 Politics and marketing

The ability of a company to market effectively in a foreign country is heavily dependent on the political, legal and regulatory environment.[7] Political factors will influence the local government's attitude to the company. Legal provisions will determine how the company will conduct business in the target market. And the regulatory environment will govern what products or services are permissible, what standards they have to meet and how they can be marketed.

Politics is a crucial factor in the conduct of international trade. Characteristics such as political stability, the attitude of political leaders to foreigners or foreign trade, or the degree of state intervention in the economy will all affect both the ability of companies to enter a foreign market and the feasibility of doing so. Much government action influences the operation of market mechanisms either in a positive or negative manner.

Moreover, with the international political context changing continuously, it is imperative that the political situation (current and potential) in any target market be well understood. Finally, companies should also remember that the Canadian government and its relationship with the target country may also play a role. In some cases, Canadian diplomatic and commercial personnel can help to support a company's business activities abroad.

6.2 Rules and regulations

When seeking to do business in another country, companies should investigate the specific regulations that will affect the conduct of their business. Figure 5 summarizes some of the key areas that can affect business operations.

---

[7] A good discussion on this topic is found in: FITTskills, *International Marketing: Participant's Manual*, (Ottawa: Forum for International Trade Training, revised 2002), pp. 91-100.

Figure 5: Regulations affecting business

Fiscal legislation	<ul><li>tax rates and tax reporting and collection practices</li><li>impact of tax treaties with foreign governments on the company and on its competitors</li><li>customs documents required</li><li>customs clearance practices</li><li>excise duties and tariffs</li></ul>
Pricing	<ul><li>wage controls</li><li>price controls</li><li>caps on profits</li></ul>
Business environment	<ul><li>business registration</li><li>competition policy (monopolies, controls on market share)</li><li>anti-dumping legislation</li><li>foreign investment legislation</li><li>business hours</li></ul>
Standards	<ul><li>technical standards</li><li>environmental requirements</li><li>health and safety legislation</li><li>restrictions on hazardous products</li><li>labelling and packaging requirements</li></ul>
Conditions of employment	<ul><li>labour laws</li><li>minimum wage legislation</li><li>equal opportunity policies</li><li>protection of human rights</li><li>work permits</li><li>professional qualification and certification</li></ul>
Intellectual property	<ul><li>copyrights</li><li>trademarks</li><li>patents</li></ul>

There may be specific political, legal or regulatory provisions that will directly affect a company's marketing activities.

- **Political** – some countries may frown on activities that North Americans see as integral to effective marketing. This may be the case with public opinion surveys. Governments that are more autocratic may be suspicious of such surveys and either prohibit them outright or impede the company's ability to carry them out. In some countries, media such as television is state-owned and financed so that it does not carry advertising.

- **Legal** – in some countries, the law may preclude or prohibit certain forms of marketing. For example, pyramid schemes are outlawed in Canadian law while contests, lotteries and giveaways are controlled.

- **Regulatory** – in some countries, the content of advertising is regulated. For example, it may not be possible to make certain claims (a product is the best), or it may not be possible to compare one product with another. In Canada, efforts are being made to deal with the flood of unsolicited ("junk") mail, either by changing postal practices or by allowing consumers to opt out of receiving such mail.

- **Immigration** – do you need a visa for a business visit? The EU, Japan, Korea, Hong Kong and Taiwan normally do not require visas for visiting Canadians. The United States, due to terrorist threats, is changing its requirements. Although, normally Canadians do not require a printed visa for a business visit to the United States, it is best to check the current situation before leaving on a trip. Issuance of foreign visas to Canadians is very easy. Visa services provided by organizations like Visa Connection make doors worldwide open quickly.

  www.visaconnection.com

If you are planning to send Canadian staff to manage or supervise an event, a project, or a larger operation such as the establishment of a branch office or a manufacturing facility in the United States, investigate American immigration regulations well in advance. Check NAFTA regulations carefully (or call the closest US consulate or border crossing) before planning to send Canadian staff to operate a US project.

Make sure your company is prepared. A good place to start is the Team Canada Inc export diagnostic (mentioned in other workshops). This is a 30-minute online questionnaire that helps to highlight issues requiring greater attention.

www.exportdiagnostic.ca

6.3   Highlights

- **An exporter's ability to market effectively in a foreign country depends heavily on the political, legal and regulatory environment.**

Case questions for discussion

1. What sort of rules and regulations will Mondetta face when operating in the US, Europe or Asia?

2. When operating in the US, will Mondetta face different regulations than in Canada?

3. What about your firm? What different regulations have you had to face in NAFTA and overseas markets?

7. Marketing the Right Product or Service

Objectives

The objectives for this chapter are as follows:

- **Identify the characteristics of a product or service that may have to be modified to satisfy the needs of the target market.**

- **Explain the advantages and disadvantages of standardization.**

- **Outline product adaptation strategies that will satisfy the target market and respect the company's objectives.**

7.1 The limitations of marketing

Clever marketing is no substitute for having the product or service that customers need. The first priority for any firm, therefore, is to make sure that it is marketing the right thing. Satisfying customers is challenging enough in a single familiar domestic market but it can be quite daunting when addressing multiple markets, each driven by a unique set of factors.

You may need help in determining whether your product/service is suited to the intended foreign market or needs to be adapted. A good place to start is the export diagnostic:

www.exportdiagnostic.ca

Companies entering foreign markets must ensure that their products and services are appropriate to those markets. In some cases, the same product can easily be offered to the entire world; Coca-Cola is a product that has succeeded in a wide variety of different markets. In other cases, an otherwise successful product simply will not work in a particular market; McDonald's entry into India was accompanied by the recognition that it could not sell beef hamburgers in a country where the cow is considered sacred. Also there is a large Muslim population in India, so pork was not an option. Instead, McDonald's sells chicken and soy burgers.

One of the most important questions facing an exporter is the question of whether or not to offer the same product or service to all markets. Alternatively, should the product or service be modified, adapted or customized to match the special needs and nuances of different markets?

Many business people have responded to the challenge of globalization by thinking of the world as a single market. Some go so far as to advocate global standardization of products. Although this approach may be tempting for those looking for economies of scale, it is not always a wise strategy, given the diversity of tastes and preferences around the globe.

There are similarities and important differences in the marketing of products and services. The following comparison (Figure 6) is drawn from Team Canada Inc's Step-by-Step Guide to Exporting.

Figure 6: Comparison of goods and services marketing

Factor	Service Exporters	Goods Exporters
Demonstrations	Presentation on capabilities	Sample product
Initial marketing by	Firm's principals	Sales representatives
Stages of marketing	Two: the firm, then service	One: the product
Local market presence	Service industry	Distributors, marketers
Exporters information needs		
Cultural factors	Interpersonal dynamics	Product colours and packaging
Local associations	Service industry	Distributors, marketers
Local events	Conferences (as speaker)	Trade shows
Media	Press coverage of firm	Advertising of product
Local partners	Other service firms	Production/distribution firms
Government procurement practices	Services contracts	Goods acquisition

7.2   Standardizing the product or service

A standardized product is one that is marketed in more than one country without any modifications. A standardized strategy is based on the belief that consumers share some common values, beliefs and consumption patterns. In deciding between standardization or modification, a company's choice of product or service strategy depends on many considerations, including potential demand, the cost of modifications, the specific requests of buyers, the nature of the competition and the potential profit to be made.

The advantages of standardization include:

- economies of scale in production, stock control, sourcing of components, training and servicing;

- a standardized product or service is a key component of a standard marketing mix;

- rapid recovery of investments made in developing the product or service; and

- easier organizational, managerial and control procedures.

Some of the disadvantages of standardization include:

- loss of marketing flexibility in foreign markets (an inability to match the product or service to specific local requirements);

- discouraging creativity and innovation, especially among local personnel; and

- loss of personnel as a result of a built-in lack of incentive to innovate.

An exporter must look at both advantages and disadvantages of standardization before deciding on an export strategy. This decision can determine the pattern and success of the firm's marketing efforts for years to come.

7.3   Product adaptation and the market environment

Foreign agents or representatives of an exporting company will often ask for product modifications to please their customers. However, the exporter should ensure that the requested modifications are realistic and the market is large enough to justify the costs of adaptation. A manufacturer should agree to modifications only after comparing the final price of the product with that of the competition.

Canadian kitchen cabinets have a reputation for high quality, but the sizes and shapes don't always fit in overseas markets, especially Japan. Japanese kitchen cabinet specifications call for lower counters and several other special characteristics. Japanese homebuilders who buy Canadian kitchen cabinets want the product modified to meet local conditions. The kitchen sinks also have to be modified. Japanese kitchen sinks have a special removable waste collection basket for vegetable shavings, choppings, clippings and leftovers pieces. The North American equivalent just doesn't do the job. Canadian kitchen cabinet manufacturers who make these modifications in their production line for Japan have good sales potential; those who don't make the modifications find that sales do not materialize.

The decision to adapt a product is also partly based on the degree of commitment to the specific foreign market, since a firm with short-term goals may have a perspective different than that of a firm with long-term goals.

One of the most important adaptations is for electrical current. Canadian manufacturers need to be aware of electrical current requirements. Foreign manufacturers of products such as stereo equipment often have a voltage switch on the product. Canadian manufacturers seldom do this. A Canadian manufacturer of prefab cabins shipped some units to a golf course project in Dalian, China. Included in the package were some Canadian light fixtures, 110 volts. China uses 220 volts. The fixtures were useless. Canadian manufacturers need to be aware of such differences and adapt their products accordingly.

Many of the following factors have to be accounted for in designing a product for a particular foreign market:

- Size – when blue jeans were first exported to Japan, only North American sizes were sent. Japanese body shapes are different and the jeans did not fit;

- Packaging preferences – some countries sell cigarettes in packs of five, 10 or individually;

- Quality;

- Appearance – labelling must be tough and attractive because in some countries, products with scratched labels will not sell;

- Where and how an item is purchased – in Quebec for example (as in many countries), beer can be purchased in supermarkets;

- Translation of slogans;

- Taste – the Japanese desire for beautiful packaging has led exporters to redesign cartons and packages specifically for that market;

- Ingredients may be subject to import controls as in the case of artificial dyes and flavourings;

- Regulations governing recycling of packaging materials;

- Prohibited ingredients such as alcohol in Muslim countries and beef or pork in India; and

- Colours and shapes.

Apart from these and the factors listed in the previous section, the international marketer must look at the following issues before deciding whether to adapt the product or not:

- **Profitability** – assess whether there is profit to be made in adapting the product. (Will likely increases in sales and possibly price justify the cost of adaptation?) The manufacturer almost always absorbs product adaptation costs.

- **Culture** – the customers' values, culture, expectations and preferences, such as use of leisure time, religion, tastes, attitudes and traditions, are crucial. In Brazil, Dunkin' Donuts are marketed as snacks, desserts and party foods because Brazilians rarely eat breakfast.

- **Local competition** – monitoring the features of competitors' products is important in order to preempt them and produce goods and services (including pre-sale, post-sale, repair services) that are harder to duplicate in the foreign market.

- **Economic conditions of target country** – the ability of foreign customers to buy products often depends on economic conditions and standards of living. Some key economic factors are:

  - purchasing power and class structure;

  - level of education;

  - general level of technical skills and maintenance standards, which might lead to product simplification (e.g. General Motors of Canada made several thousand Chevrolets for a Middle East country and took out many standard features which were not required);

- local labour costs (affects higher or lower degree of automation);

- energy costs (affects the demand for a country's energy consuming products);

- availability of resources; and

- standard of living (if a country's standard of living is lower than the exporting country's, a manufacturer may find a market for a product which has become almost obsolete in the domestic market).

Many companies have successfully adapted existing products to address different markets. For example, a gadget designed for the hand washing of clothes, a mangle, had reached the end of its product life in the United Kingdom in the late 1960s with the advent of washing machines with a spin cycle. However, market research showed that there were millions of women in South America who still washed clothes by hand. This product was adapted for use in rural settings and marketed successfully in Argentina, Brazil and other parts of South America.

7.4   Adaptation of services

Services destined for export must also suit the target market. Indeed, it may be more likely that exported services will have to be adapted to local conditions. Consulting engineers and architects will have to take local standards and norms into account. Providers of business services will have to adapt to local business culture. Trainers and educators may have to adopt different pedagogical techniques. And all providers of services will be affected by linguistic and cultural difference, perhaps to an even greater degree than the providers of goods.

This does not mean that there are no global service providers. Airlines and couriers offer their services worldwide. And there are many consulting companies and law firms that have offices in many different countries. Even so, such companies have become successful because they have managed to strike an effective balance between offering an international service and doing so in a way that appeals to the unique sensibilities of each market.

7.5   Some adaptation strategies

It is generally accepted that international product modification should be considered in conjunction with the message being sent about the product. In devising the export market strategy, the bottom line of profit should be kept in mind, along with the resources available (e.g. capital, personnel, production facilities).

Companies have several export-market product strategies available to them depending on their needs and market objectives.

- **Same product, same message** – Coca-Cola and Levi Strauss are companies that use this approach. It is appropriate when the product fills similar needs and is used in a similar way abroad and at home.

- **Same product, different message** – this strategy is used where the product serves different needs or is used differently in the foreign market. Bicycles are recreational items in North America but they provide basic transportation in China, India and Holland.

- **Different product, same message** – Esso adjusted its gasoline to the different weather conditions throughout the world but still uses the same promotional message.

- **Dual adaptation** – this involves changing both the product and the message to reflect differences in both product function and use. This strategy tends to be expensive.

- **Invention** – this involves new product development, for example when customers cannot afford a product because of the lower standard of living in that marketplace or when cheaper manufacturing technology can be used to fulfill the same need.

7.6   Highlights

- **Clever marketing is no substitute for having the product or services that the customer needs.**

- **A standardized product may be suited to customers that share common values, beliefs and consumption patterns.**

- **Adapting a product will be subject to considerations such as profitability, competition and culture.**

Case questions for discussion

1. Do we know if Mondetta has modified its sizes and styles for offshore markets? What strategies should they adopt to do the above?

2. Has your company adapted its product or service for an overseas target market?

8. Personal Selling in International Marketing

Objectives

The objectives for this chapter are as follows:

- **Explain the preparation and planning required to ensure a successful foreign business trip.**

- **Outline the role of visits, trade missions and fairs in a company's international marketing strategy.**

8.1 What is personal selling?

Every business engages in personal selling, regardless of its sector or the nature of its offerings. Companies use personal contact and face-to-face negotiation to make deals with distributors, engage representatives, enter into partnerships, secure financing or finalize sales contracts. In each of these instances, the success of the transaction depends on the ability of the individual involved to market the strengths and capabilities of his or her company.

Personal selling is probably far more common than the more visible marketing campaigns aimed at mass audiences. Not every company produces for the mass market. But every company will have to deal with suppliers, distributors, partners, agents, brokers and buyers for some significant portion of its activities.

Personal selling is usually involved when companies move outside the domestic arena. In fact, it is probably the very first marketing they do abroad. New exporters may make exploratory trips into foreign markets. They may meet with leads and contacts. And many of them will participate in trade shows or go on trade missions. The common feature of all of these activities is face-to-face contact with a potential client, and thus the need for personal selling.

Sales visits, trade missions and trade fairs are marketing activities characterized by direct personal contact. Visits, missions and fairs can be used to gather market intelligence, establish personal contacts, promote awareness of the company and its offerings, or make sales.

Most Canadian companies embarking on international trade will use some combination of sales visits, missions and fairs as part of their marketing. A number of government programs and services are available to help them in these activities.

8.2 Business trips to foreign markets

Personal selling means travelling. In the international context, this involves addressing the challenges of distance, crossing national borders, dealing in different languages and accommodating cultural differences. All of this makes international travel expensive, time consuming, disruptive and tiring.

Senior executives do it, however, because from a marketing perspective, there is no alternative to personal contact in the following areas:

- following up on leads and building new relationships;

- gathering market intelligence and assessing opportunities;

- raising awareness of a company and its capabilities;

- conducting various types of negotiations and finalizing agreements;

- making sales and taking orders; and

- addressing client concerns and complaints.

To realize all of these benefits, however, the potential exporter must prepare carefully. Personal selling involves planning, preparation and concentration on taking advantage of existing relationships and contacts.

Objectives of the business trip

A successful business trip starts with clear objectives. The following are some of the reasons for visiting a foreign market:

- **Market assessment** – many business travellers want to confirm that there really are opportunities for their company in a target market. They also want to gather details about the market (e.g. size, trends, receptivity).

- **Exploring business conditions** – even attractive markets may not be accessible. A personal visit can help to determine if there are political or regulatory barriers to market entry, if appropriate infrastructure exists, if the business climate is favourable and if trade is feasible.

- **Determining product/service suitability** – few products or services can be introduced into foreign markets without any change whatsoever. Personal visits may be needed to determine exactly what adjustments are required to make a company's offerings acceptable and attractive in a target market.

- **Competitor intelligence** – companies need to know what competition exists in a market before committing to it. Are similar products or services available? How strong is the competition? Can the exporting firm match those strengths?

- **Developing leads** – new exporters may have been given some leads or may wish to find others. They may also want to make contact with those that can help them enter the market.

- **Risk assessment** – a visit can help inform an exporter about the various risks associated with a business venture.

- **Strategic planning** – a personal visit can be invaluable in developing a market entry strategy or a marketing campaign.

There are many other reasons for business travel such as attending a trade show or an international exposition (such as the Aichi Expo 2005 in Japan). If you have customers or clients in the Nagoya area, they will be impressed that you took the time to visit "their" expo.

www.expo2005.or.jp

Trade missions are often the first exposure that a company executive will have to a particular market. Follow-up trips to that market might include the signing of a Memorandum of Understanding or later on a contract.

Before getting on a plane, business people must be clear as to what they hope to achieve during a trip. They should know who they want to meet, for what purpose and with what result. They should also be clear about what information they can access from home and what can be gathered only on location in the target market. And they should have precise criteria by which they can tell whether or not the trip has successfully achieved its objectives.

There are many examples of companies that fail to prepare adequately, have no clear idea of what they hoped to achieve, and thus waste time and money on pointless travel. Moreover, a company that blunders on its first foray into a market may not get another chance. There is a network of Canadian trade commissioners, bilateral business groups and trade centres that can be used to access most of the world's most promising markets.

However, a poorly prepared company that has abused these resources (or embarrassed them before people from the host country) may find it very difficult to get a second hearing.

Preparing for a foreign business trip

International Trade Canada (ITCan) makes a point of encouraging business people to prepare carefully before travelling abroad. To emphasize the importance of serious preparation, ITCan mentions that at least two-thirds of the work involved in personal selling abroad can and should be done right here in Canada, usually from the business person's desk.

The ITCan web site will give you much up-to-date travel information and is a good place to start planning your business trip. Follow the links from:

www.itcan.gc.ca.

Also, Team Canada Inc has an online guide called *Planning a Business Trip Abroad* which is available at:

www.exportsource.ca/trip.

Once business objectives have been defined, research is conducted in support of those objectives. This may involve gathering information about the target market, and then about the firms, stakeholders and decision makers active in that market.

There are many sources that can be used during this initial research phase, such as the following:

- the Internet (web sites such as ExportSource (**www.exportsource.ca**), Strategis (**www.strategis.gc.ca**) or the ITCan site (**www.itcan.gc.ca**) contain a wealth of information about foreign markets as well as links to other sources of market information);

- other Canadian firms that have experience in the target market;

- bilateral business councils dedicated to expanding trade between Canada and the target country;

- Team Canada Inc;

- Canadian Trade Commissioner Service desk officers responsible for the target country;

- chambers of commerce or boards of trade;

- sectoral business associations (for identifying companies active in foreign markets).

It may also be useful to find out if there are trade missions being organized from Canada into the target market (or from the target country to Canada). Many new exporters get their first taste of a foreign market by participating in such missions.

The preliminary research will take some time. If it is done well, it will be possible to define what the company expects as an outcome from the trip. At this point, the company may attempt to make contact with the Canadian trade commissioner service at the post in the target country.

Most Canadian embassies abroad have their own web sites. Additional information can be found by visiting **www.itcan.gc.ca** and selecting "Our Offices Abroad".

www.beijing.gc.ca

It should be noted that Canada's trade commissioners are extremely busy. They do not have the time to bring individual companies up to speed or to do their research for them. If they feel that a company is not ready to export, they will refer it back to institutions in Canada that can help with trade preparation.

Companies should be well informed about the target market and what they expect there before approaching the trade commissioner's office. Make sure you are well prepared, that you have done your basic market research before you go and have some idea of which companies in your target sector you would like to visit. This means having names, addresses and telephone numbers researched in advance.

Planning a business trip

Once you have a good idea of your overall objectives, you can start making travel preparations.

- **Plan itinerary** – once you know who you want to visit, you can start juggling itineraries and schedules. Where are your targets located? When are they available? What is the best way of meeting all of them? What connections are available between Canada and the target country? Are discounts available for booking early?

- **Hotel reservations** – for business travellers, hotels are not just places to sleep. They are also places to do work and hold meetings. Make sure that accommodations are suitable for business purposes, especially if some meetings with clients have to be held at the hotel. Apart from price and availability, the traveller should also check location and see about additional facilities such as faxes, Internet connections and meeting rooms. The better hotels provide fully-equipped business centres for the use of their guests.

- **Travel documents** – travellers need a valid Canadian passport to travel to all countries apart from the United States. However, US authorities have recently made their requirements much stricter. The most important formality on entering the United States is providing proof of Canadian citizenship. In order to avoid possible problems, all Canadians should carry a Canadian passport for all visits to the United States.

  www.voyage.gc.ca/main/pubs/usa_bound-en.asp

  Many countries also require a travel visa issued by their consulates. Visitors going to some countries (especially in the tropics) will need a health certificate and/or immunization. Health documents may be needed for entry into the target country and admission back into Canada.

- **Business cards and marketing materials** – business cards and promotional materials (including diskettes, CD-ROMs and videotapes) describing the company (preferably in the language of the target country) should be prepared well in advance and any translations verified. If you have videos, make sure they are in the right format for the country and are in the right language (e.g. Cantonese for Hong Kong and Mandarin for China and Taiwan). If the traveller wishes to take samples or personal equipment (e.g. computers, audio-visual equipment), a Carnet will be required to allow passage through Customs without duties being charged.

- **Contact the Canadian officials in the country** – once travel plans are advanced, the visitor should contact the Canadian officials posted in the countries to be visited. This is more than a courtesy. In some cases, these officials can help to arrange and confirm appointments with prospects. In other cases, their help will be invaluable in dealing with the government.

- **Arrange meetings** – closer to departure, the traveller should contact all prospects to finalize meetings. It is extremely important that times and places are clearly understood by both sides and that there is a way of getting in touch if plans change.

- **Study relevant cultural issues** – the business traveller should be familiar with business etiquette, practices and taboos in the target country.

- **Gifts** – in many countries, it is customary to present small gifts to contacts as a token of appreciation. The purpose of these gifts should not be misunderstood, so some research is required to make sure they are appropriate.

- **Travel conditions and conducting business** – the smart traveller will find out everything possible about travelling in the target country, including:

  - climate;

- normal business attire;

- local transportation (e.g. taxis, buses, rail);

- availability of translation services;

- local currency, convertibility, exchange rates;

- departure, arrival, airport procedures, customs;

- medical coverage while in target country, availability of medicines;

- food, restaurants, dining tips;

- phone, fax, Internet, computer, electrical outlets, power sources;

- normal business hours and national holidays;

- procedures to follow in case of robbery or other crime;

- attitude toward Canadians in the country;

- social customs, behaviour, greetings, gestures, conversation;

- how business negotiations are conducted;

- how to respond to invitations to social functions;

- background information on the country, history, politics, etc.; and

- the best sources of any information that must be collected during the trip.

- **Currency** – where possible, the traveller should take sufficient local currency for the trip. It is now possible to use Canadian credit cards and bank cards in many countries, but this should be investigated before departure. Additional money can be carried in traveller's cheques. If the traveller is carrying cash, US currency is preferred to the less familiar Canadian dollar.

Things to do during the trip

While each trip is unique, the following are examples of the types of tasks that a business traveller may perform during the course of a foreign visit:

- meet potential customers;

- determine suitability of company's products or services;

- confirm market size and growth;

- determine appropriate pricing;

- obtain competitor intelligence;

- identify potential agents and distributors;

- validate financial and business strengths of prospective partners;

- investigate and locate storage and distribution facilities;

- identify local resource people;

- locate legal and accounting services;

- gather information about local regulations and requirements;

- investigate protection offered on intellectual property;

- gather information about shipping, marking, labelling, documentation, tariffs and possible non-tariff barriers; and

- gather market research (e.g. customer profiles, income levels, tastes and preferences, how purchasing decisions are made, how sales are made).

After the trip

The effort and expense put into a trip abroad may be wasted unless there is appropriate follow-up. At a minimum, the traveller should write to those with whom he or she met, and to those who helped in making arrangements. If promises were made (e.g. to provide additional information), these should be carried out. Follow-up, living up to promises made, and communication is the best way to develop new networks to facilitate business now and in the future.

In fact, it is a good idea while still meeting with prospects in the target country to agree to an explicit set of next steps following the meeting. These should then form the basis of all follow-up activities once the trip is concluded.

8.3   Trade shows and exhibitions

Successful selling is an exercise in effective communications between two or more human beings. While the product or service being sold is important, the first priority in any sales effort is to establish a communications link between the buyer and seller. Trade shows and exhibitions are an effective way of initiating that communication where no other link has existed.

The following web sites offer a good introduction to trade shows and can save a considerable amount of planning time and effort:

Successful International Trade Show Marketing:

www.exportsource.ca/tradeshow

Team Canada Inc Missions:

www.teamcanada.gc.ca

Trade Show Central:

www2.tsnn.com

A very good book on trade shows is Barry Siskind's, *The Power of Exhibit Marketing.* This book presents the various stages of attending and participating at a trade show. It is available from:

www.siskindtraining.com

Three forms of participation in a fair are common. First, companies can attend as visitors to view the competition, assess the market and develop a list of contacts for later follow-up. Second, companies can participate as exhibitors, raising awareness, developing contacts and enhancing prestige. Third, companies can participate in panel discussions or make a presentation. Many trade fairs also feature speakers and workshops as part of their activities. By securing a speaking invitation, companies can get profile without incurring the expenses of exhibition.

Fairs can be classified in various ways and do not always fit neatly into categories. Some fairs are narrowly focused on a specific industrial sector or type of product. Others will address virtually any type of business. Some fairs are exhibitions, at which participants can show what they have to offer. Others are real markets at which it is expected that those attending will come to make purchases from participants.

Most fairs fall under one of the following headings: major general fairs, major specialized trade fairs, secondary trade fairs and consumer fairs.

- **Major general fairs** – all kinds of consumer and industrial goods are exhibited at general trade fairs. They are open to the public, but business people also attend. The audience may be international, national, regional or even provincial in scope.

- **Major specialized trade fairs** – designed primarily for business visitors, such fairs may also admit the general public, usually for only part of the time. They are specialized by industry or trade sector (e.g. food or leather), or sometimes by market (e.g. hospitals or schools). The audience can be both international and national in scope, and tends to include people from various levels of trade and industry. If a firm is trying to enter a market, these fairs offer an excellent opportunity to find an agent or importer/distributor. When a firm is established in the market, these fairs can often be used to support representatives by providing them with the opportunity to make contacts with industrial buyers and retailers.

- **Secondary trade fairs** – most trade fairs fall under this category. Although they do not rank with the major fairs, they can be very important in their respective fields. They include highly-specialized exhibitions, national or even international in scope, as well as many regional and provincial specialized exhibitions. They are usually restricted to business visitors, and many of the regional or provincial exhibitions are aimed specifically at retailers.

- **Consumer fairs** – these events are intended primarily for the general public, either from the immediate area or from various parts of the country. Most of these fairs are general with respect to products shown and areas of audience interest.

World expositions

World expositions, or expos as they are popularly called, are the granddaddies of all trade shows. In theory, expos are cultural expositions where each country displays the best of their best. However, expos are really giant trade shows where companies make sure their names are known and countries show off their science and technology. Some expos such as Tsukuba and Vancouver focused on more specific themes: science for Tsukuba and transportation for Vancouver. The theme of the Aichi, Japan Expo in 2005 will be "Nature's Wisdom".

www.expo2005canada.gc.ca

www.expo2005.or.jp

How can a small- to medium-sized Canadian company, either exporting or wanting to export, participate in a trade show alongside the giants? The answer is corporate sponsorships. The Canadian pavilion at any world fair (expo) is always looking for suitable sponsorships. Things like hosting staff uniforms can be sponsored. The VIP lounge is always looking for Canadian products to present to VIP visitors. One Canadian jam producer found their product could be used in the VIP lounge. A flag maker found that a Canadian pavilion needed three sets of the flags of Canada, the provinces and territories. A beer producer's product found a ready use in the VIP lounge.

Companies that have a product that a Canadian pavilion could use, or that would like to sponsor something in the Pavilion with a cash grant, should contact the appropriate office in Ottawa and to see if they can become sponsors in a Canadian pavilion at a world expo.

The importance of trade shows and exhibitions

The main reason for attending or exhibiting at a trade show or exhibition is to increase product exposure and ultimately sales. These fairs provide a highly efficient way of meeting potential customers, seeing competitors' products or services and generally finding out what is happening in the industry.

Trade fairs provide customers with an opportunity to see the product in action. There is usually a chance to ask or answer questions and determine the extent to which potential customers are interested in a product or service. Trade fairs offer an important venue for the introduction of new products.

A large number of potential and existing buyers attend trade shows. This is a good opportunity to meet many of them and build contacts. At the same time, trade shows provide products or services with exposure to a target audience, especially if the trade fair is a vertical one. In such a fair, the product enjoys immediate exposure to many potential customers.

Trade fairs are also useful for market research. They allow a company to test customers' reaction and interest in its products or services. Because trade shows are usually well attended, products receive a great deal of exposure in a relatively short time. In addition, fairs provide excellent networking opportunities with potential clients.

Trade fairs also offer the prospective exporter an opportunity to check out the competition. It is likely that a major general or sectoral fair will attract the other companies involved in the sector, so attending the fair makes it possible not only to see what they are offering but also observe reactions to it.

Since products are displayed, trade fairs allow the customers to see and "touch" the product, and watch a demonstration of it. If a customer at the fair expresses an interest, the exhibitor has the opportunity to follow up with a meeting or to visit the customer's premises.

Selecting the right trade show or exhibition

Tens of thousands of commercial events are held around the world and virtually every country hosts at least a few of them. One way of sorting through what is available is through the Internet.

Trade Show Central is a free Internet service providing information on more than 30,000 trade shows, conferences and seminars, 5,000 service providers, and 5,000 venues and facilities around the world. TSCentral connects people who organize and support trade shows with those who attend and exhibit at them. It can be accessed at **www.tscentral.com**.

Despite the many benefits of attending trade fairs, there are some disadvantages to consider. Attending and exhibiting at trade fairs is costly in terms of extra time and the expenses of setting up a booth or exhibit. If a company has decided to participate in trade fairs as a marketing vehicle, it is important that it choose the right fairs to attend.

To evaluate a fair, it is also important to obtain as much information as possible about the exhibitors, and what kinds of products they show. Exporters should aim for a fair that shows products similar to their own. Although this will place the firm in a competitive environment, the fair is more likely to attract a large number of visitors genuinely interested in seeing such products.

Figure 7 displays a list of items that should be researched about a trade fair before registering as a visitor, exhibitor or participant.

Figure 7: Checklist for the selection of a trade fair

Name of show or exhibition	Checklist
Dates Next event Frequency (annual, biannual?)	
Type and sector Is the fair intended for a general or sector-specific audience? Is it for exhibitors only, or can sales be made to consumers?	
Attendance What were attendance figures like over the past few events? How many are expected at the next event? How many countries are represented? Who are the exhibitors? Who are the visitors?	

Name of show or exhibition	Checklist
Location of the fair Country or region of the world? Proximity to key markets? Are there other exhibit or business opportunities available in conjunction with the fair? Accessibility (e.g. ease of travel to communication with the site)?	
History When was the event founded and by whom? What is its reputation and success? Organizers (and contact names)?	
Facilities How large an area does the fair cover? What kinds of building(s) house the fair? Is it located in a town or city? How big are booths and other spaces? What other facilities are on the fairgrounds (e.g. meeting rooms, facilities for product demonstrations)? Are hotels and other accommodations nearby?	
Fees For participation? For renting a booth (rate per unit of area)? For attending as a visitor? What services are included in renting a booth? What is the cost of clearing samples? What is the cost of services not supplied by organizers? What is the cost of an interpreter if one is needed?	
Travel What modes of transportation serve the centre? What connections exist with Canada (e.g. flights, trucking services)? What is the best way of getting products and samples to the fair? What are the Customs and import regulations for products being exhibited? Are special licenses required? Can the goods be easily taken back to Canada?	

Name of show or exhibition	Checklist
Applications What are the lead times for applying as a visitor, exhibitor or participant? What procedures, restrictions or documents are involved? What is the space reservation deadline?	

Preparing for a trade show or exhibition

A successful show or exhibition, like any well-executed marketing exercise, depends on a carefully thought-out plan of action. Such a plan gives direction to the whole effort, set goals and provides yardsticks against which to measure results.

A natural beginning is to ask two preliminary questions, "Why should the firm exhibit?" and "What does the company stand to gain?" Perhaps equally important is the question, "What criteria can be used to measure success?"

The following is a list of possible objectives in attending a fair, together with some examples of how a firm can measure the extent to which it has achieved those objectives.

Figure 8: Examples of measurable objectives regarding trade fairs

Raise awareness of firm	Number of people visiting booth or the number of people attending presentation/demonstration
Secure leads and contacts	Number of people visiting booth and the number of business cards exchanged
Conduct market research	Amount and quality of information gathered
Secure contracts	Value of contract(s) initiated
Find foreign/local partners	Number of leads to potential partners, number of qualified candidates and number of candidates interviewed
Test product/service	Results of presentation/demonstration
Research reaction to product/service	Gather responses to presentation or demonstration using response cards or a focused discussion
Learn about new products/processes/technologies	Quality of information gathered
Acquire new products/processes/technologies	Number and quality of leads and contacts

A trade fair is clearly a place where companies can engage in direct and (potentially) highly effective marketing. The kinds of techniques to be used during the show will depend on both the nature of the product or service as well as the firm's objectives in attending the event.

Marketing at a trade show or exhibition can involve far more than simply manning a booth. Target clients may be identified and offered special hospitality. The firm may secure a place on the speaker's list as a way of explaining and positioning itself. In some cases, firms attract attention through the use of high-profile gimmicks. If the objective is to find leads or take orders, special introductory offers can be associated with the event.

In planning for the trade fair, some effort should also be made to compare the desired outcomes listed in the previous figure with the likely costs of participation. A budget will have to be drawn up and the company should monitor estimated and actual expenses.

The cost of attending the trade fair may involve any or all of the following expense items:

- registration fees;

- exhibition fees (if applicable);

- travel documents (e.g. fees for passports, visas);

- special permits, Carnets for samples;

- travel to and from destination;

- incidental travel (e.g. taxis, parking, car rentals);

- accommodation (e.g. hotel, meals, per diems, incidentals);

- hospitality (e.g. for clients, contacts);

- costs of display booth, transport, set-up, dismantling, return transportation;

- special equipment for demonstrations or presentations (e.g. display screens, VCRs, computers, slide projectors, overhead projectors);

- brochures and other printed materials (including design, translation and printing costs);

- business cards (translated into local language, reprinted if necessary);

- production of samples, software for demonstrations;

- additional staff (if necessary) to maintain booth, demonstrate products; and

- training of additional or existing staff.

In addition to drawing up a budget, other activities involved in the preparation will include:

- deciding who will staff the exhibit;

- securing a desirable location at the show;

- consulting early with an exhibit designer;

- all travel-related issues;

- obtaining the necessary export license for promotional products;

- learning about specific foreign business practices, taking appropriate steps to bridge the language barrier;

- finding out about protection of intellectual property;

- learning about credit and payment methods;

- initiating promotional activities in advance.

The task of developing the show materials and getting the booth prepared can be demanding. A number of organizations within the federal and provincial governments provide assistance in planning for a trade show.

Once the show or exhibition starts, more steps have to be taken by the exhibitor to ensure success. They include:

- arriving early, staying late;

- keeping the exhibit staffed at all times;

- learning everything possible from other exhibitors;

- selecting good overseas representatives;

- being able to quote price, delivery time and terms;

- remembering that samples can generate sales;

- training and evaluating company representatives;

- using service representatives at fairs;

- following up all leads.

The follow-up includes keeping in contact with customers and servicing the foreign clients.

The following checklist can help develop a critical path for participating in a trade show. It identifies the key milestones involved in preparing for a show. These should be set against dates by which certain tasks must be completed. The exact order of tasks will vary from one event to another.

Figure 9: Checklist for foreign trade fairs

Task	Details	Start	Completion Date
Research	Find out about the fair, who will be there, costs, potential benefits, etc.	12 months before	
Draw up action plan	▪ List of key steps ▪ Budget	12 months before	
Secure advice	Talk to: ▪ event organizers; ▪ experienced Canadian firms; ▪ Canadian officials (e.g. ITCan); ▪ members of bilateral business councils; ▪ embassy staff or trade commissioners in host country. Inform Canadian trade commissioner of your exhibit plans and keep ongoing information and relevant correspondence flowing.	12-9 months before	
Leads	Develop list of leads and contacts by talking to: ▪ officials at ITCan, Canadian International Development Agency, etc.; ▪ members of a relevant bilateral business council; ▪ embassy or trade commission of the host country; ▪ Canadian firms doing business in the target market; in-country trade commissioners. This list of leads and contacts will confirm whether or not the fair is worth attending.	12-9 months before	
Registrations	▪ As exhibitor ▪ As visitor ▪ Mail contracts for trade fair and send reservation deposits	Depends on event	

Task	Details	Start	Completion Date
Applications	<ul><li>Carnet for samples</li><li>Special permits (safety, health, etc.)</li><li>Passport updated (if necessary) for all attendees</li><li>Visa (if necessary) for all attendees</li><li>Health and immunization documentation</li></ul>	6 months before	
Define strategy	<ul><li>Brainstorming to define approach, main messages, differentiation strategy</li><li>Plan your exhibit and booth space and, if possible, try to include an office space in which to conduct business</li><li>Decide whether you will design, construct or set up your own exhibit or employ consultants, then finalize arrangements for this</li><li>Decide what samples will be required and ensure they will be available</li></ul>	6 months before	
Display equipment and booth	<ul><li>Define requirements</li><li>Source from within, rent or purchase</li><li>Test assembly and disassembly</li></ul>	4 months before	
Promotional materials	<ul><li>Decide on pre-fair publicity, public relations, literature, promotional material, who will produce and translate it and finalize arrangements</li><li>Develop any demonstrations, presentations, software, videos, brochures, business cards, etc. that might be required for the show</li><li>This includes planning, writing, translation, layout and design, proofing and production</li></ul>	4 months before	
Shipping	<ul><li>Determine what needs to be shipped (samples, booth, display equipment, etc.) and what can accompany the team</li><li>Arrange for shipping in time for fair</li><li>Make sure all materials to be shipped are available on time</li></ul>	3 months before	

Task	Details	Start	Completion Date
Staff	▪ Assess staffing requirements in country (managing booth, product demonstrations, marketing, etc.) ▪ Hire support staff (if necessary) ▪ Provide relevant training on company and its products and services	3 months before	
Display equipment and booth	▪ Finalize the team that will go overseas ▪ Airplane reservations ▪ Hotel accommodations ▪ Departure and arrival procedures ▪ Customs procedures for accompanying samples and equipment	2 months before	
Rehearsals	Dry runs and critiques of: ▪ presentations ▪ demonstrations ▪ marketing approach	1 month before	

Materials required for trade shows and exhibitions

Business cards

The single most important tool for personal selling is a business card. Business cards should be printed on both sides, with one side carrying a translation into the language of the target market.

An Ottawa bureaucrat was transferred to a new job in Vancouver. His secretary asked him if he would like bilingual business cards. Pleased that a business centre so far from central Canada thought bilingual cards were important, he immediately said yes. The next day his secretary told him she had received a call from the printer. "Would you like your cards in Japanese or Chinese?"

In some countries, there is an elaborate etiquette involved in the presentation of business cards. This should be well understood before undertaking the visit.

A Pacific Rim trade consultant, temporarily working in Toronto, was horrified when an advertising executive, making a pitch for some business, threw his business card across the table to the consultant. Because throwing the card was taken as an expression of disrespect, the executive did not make a very good impression and did not get the business.

Promotional kit

Regardless of what material is developed for a visit, mission or trade show, a basic printed promotional kit with a theme should be prepared for all media use. It is integral to the sales process.

The kit contains background information on the company, a product catalogue with illustrations, photographs and testimonials, and compelling examples of how the product or service has helped other clients. Price lists, delivery schedule and terms of payment are best printed separately to accommodate constant changes within these areas.

The kit should be sent ahead to prospective clients before leaving on a foreign sales mission. It will give potential buyers time to review the products and check out a firm's credit worthiness and references. This builds credibility.

The kit should be printed in English or French and in the language spoken in the chosen market. Translations will need special attention to avoid potentially embarrassing and costly mistakes. Poor translations, especially with technical and semi-technical instructional material, may confuse the reader and also can have legal implications.

It is a good idea to design and write your copy with translation in mind. Avoid slang or any unusual expressions. Bear in mind that languages spoken in more than one country show great variation nationally and regionally.

Translation should include conversions from inches to centimetres, gallons to litres or vice versa. Many experienced export marketers have had good results actually producing such material in the target country.

In non-English- and non-French-speaking countries, examine the meaning and acceptability of brand names and logos used in Canada. Make sure that no negative or inappropriate connotations are conveyed. Make sure that colour symbols used in promotional material are sensitive to local tastes and consumer preferences.

Samples

In some cases, product samples are an effective selling tool. Special permits, admission temporaire – temporary admission (ATA) Carnets, will be needed to get commercial samples across international borders without duty.

www.chamber.ca/article.asp?id=259

www.atacarnet.com

The following is a US site with some useful information on carnets.

www.uscib.org/index.asp?documentID=718

Other permits may be needed in the cases of dangerous goods, controlled substances, certain foodstuffs or materials posing a health or safety hazard.

Other marketing aids

A host of other materials could be useful in promoting a product or service. These include videotapes, audiocassettes, CD-ROMs and diskettes. Indeed, today's electronic technology has largely superseded some older promotional forms such as 35 mm slides.

It should also be recalled that a considerable amount of marketing is now done on the Internet. A corporate web site can be a powerful complement to participation in a trade show.

Sources of financial assistance for trade shows and exhibitions

Financial assistance is available to companies that are using international travel as part of foreign market development.

8.4 Highlights

- The success of a transaction may depend on the ability of the individual involved to market the strengths and capabilities of the company.

- Personal selling involves travelling.

- A successful business trip starts with clear objectives, requires planning, preparation and a follow-up.

- The main reason for attending or exhibiting at a trade show is to increase product exposure and sales.

Case questions for discussion

1. If Mondetta is planning to exhibit at a trade show in Milan, what languages should their literature be in?

2. Should the Mondetta representatives' business cards be in several languages – if so which ones?

3. Has your firm participated in a trade show in Europe or in Asia? What special preparations did you make for brochures and business cards?

9. Pricing and International Marketing

Objectives

The objectives for this chapter are as follows:

- **Explain the different pricing strategies to consider in preparing a company's international marketing strategy.**

- **List the costs to include when establishing an export price for a product.**

- **Identify the pricing strategy that fits within a company's international marketing strategy.**

9.1 The role of prices in marketing

Prices are an important factor in helping companies achieve their marketing objectives. If a company has no long-term plans for a particular foreign market and there is an opportunity to sell a single or occasional export order, it may be acceptable for it to use its existing domestic price list.

On the other hand, if the company is concerned with developing long-term sales and profits, more thoughtful approaches are appropriate. This is particularly true when using a foreign distributor network, where special pricing skills are in order. Pricing is always intimately linked to marketing; even the cleverest marketing will fail if the price is not right.

Pricing varies depending upon the marketing objectives being pursued. Where the company is trying to establish itself in a fiercely competitive market, it may consider sacrificing short-term profits in the hope of gaining long-term market share. In introducing products that are entirely new to markets in developing countries, gaining market acceptance and building the market may be the important concerns. In such cases, low initial prices would encourage buying and build familiarity.

In some countries, a firm may just want to maintain a position until it is ready for the next push. Moderate pricing should be used to support such an objective.

At other times, a company may want to gain a temporary sales boost to absorb overheads or smooth out seasonal sale fluctuations. Clearing obsolete inventory may be a priority at other times. Such situations call for temporary sales at lower-than-normal prices.

Finally, companies that have spent significant sums on R&D may be keen to recoup that investment as quickly as possible. In such cases, they may charge high prices, and customers may be willing to pay the premium to be among the first to try a new or improved product.

Later, as the experimental product becomes familiar, as the company learns how to make it more efficiently, and as competitors and imitators crowd into the market, the company will drop its prices.

This type of pricing trajectory is quite familiar in technology-driven products such as computers and consumer electronics.

In addition to company objectives, pricing decisions are also influenced by the nature of the business and various market factors. These influences include costs, competition, supply and demand, distribution, product development cycles and regulatory considerations. It must also be remembered that price interconnects with all areas of marketing, such as personal sales, promotion, level of service, product quality, delivery, consumer perception and product loyalty.

9.2   Pricing strategies

The factors influencing price setting are directly linked with a company's marketing strategy. In other words, the pricing strategy chosen will depend on the firm's marketing objectives. The following are some possibilities:

- Is the firm entering a new market and looking to get noticed and accepted? If so, it should probably charge a low introductory price.

- Is the firm looking to position itself in a particular way? If it wants to be seen in terms of luxury or quality, it should price accordingly.

- Is it seeking to maximize the market opportunity by addressing all portions of the available market? If so, it may want to price flexibly to capture every part of the market.

- Is the market so far away and so difficult that the firm wants to minimize the administrative and operational costs of selling? If so, perhaps it should charge a single price.

- Is it seeking to recoup its investments within a narrow window? If so, it should charge whatever the market will bear before competitors drive down prices.

Beyond these broad marketing strategies there are a host of day-to-day tactical concerns. For example, should discounts be offered for volume purchases? What kinds of special sales and promotions are appropriate?

Some of the more common traditional pricing strategies are summarized in the following figure.

Figure 10: Common pricing strategies

Strategy	Description
Static pricing	Charging the same price to all customers
Flexible pricing	Adjusting prices for different classes of customers
Penetration pricing	Charging low prices to secure acceptance and market share
Skimming	Charging premium prices to selected customers in order to maximize profits despite low volumes
Market maintenance	Absorbing cost increases and holding prices firm in order to maintain market share

9.3   Setting the export price

Incoterms

In setting an export price, it is important to understand the export process and what may be included or excluded in a price. That, in turn, means understanding Incoterms and what they represent. The International Chamber of Commerce in Paris first developed Incoterms in 1936 and now updates them every ten years. The last version is from 2000. See Appendices 6 and 7 for Incoterms charts and illustrations. A complete list, a reprint of the ICC Incoterms is available from the international section of most major chartered banks in Canada. Inquiries should be directed to the international section of the bank, not the local branch. For additional detail, see the following sites:

www.acdi-cida.gc.ca under Search type in "Incoterms" and refer to section 2.2.

www.iccwbo.org/index_incoterms.asp

www.incoterms-4-americans.com

www.cbsc.org/alberta/tbl.cfm?fn=incoterm

It should be noted that Incoterms are used everywhere but in the United States, where companies use American Foreign Trade Definitions, 1941. Readers should not confuse Incoterms with American Foreign Trade Definitions (AFTD). The latter are more commonly used in the US (and by certain industries in western Canada such as the lumber export industry). For more detail on US usage and how it differs from Incoterms, see:

www.mohawksyr.com/news/Oct_08_2003Whither_FOB_factory.htm

Applying Incoterms to pricing

There are many ways to export directly. Some companies calculate their profit in their EXWorks price and add marine insurance and shipping. This gives them a CIF (cost, insurance, freight) price. Other companies take their EXWorks price as a basis and then add on all handling charges, a finance charge, an export profit margin, ocean freight and marine insurance. There are even situations where a company will calculate a CIF cost and then add their profit margin on top of that, the result being their CIF price.

In *market-oriented pricing*, the setting of prices typically requires the company to have carried out market research on the market demand, the competitors and their prices, and the trends in prices. This enables the company to formulate a pricing strategy and to establish a target price.

The company must then confirm that the target price is sufficient to cover the costs, which it incurs under the strategy and that the pricing generates an acceptable profit margin. International marketers must remember that most foreign buyers of goods and services work in the global marketplace and, as a result, they demand world market prices and conditions.

In *cost-based pricing*, the emphasis is first on the establishment of prices to cover certain specified costs and to satisfy certain profit criteria. Consideration of the competitive implications follows later, but in practice is often overlooked (especially by sellers of industrial goods).

Many companies have to develop an export price when they receive an unsolicited inquiry and/or order from a foreign customer. They necessarily have to start with their EXW (EXWorks) price. Their target is to develop a competitive CIF price.[8] The final CIF price at the time of writing (2004) will most likely be in US dollars. This could change in the future since members of the EU will most likely want prices quoted in euros.

Incoterms™2000	Seller's responsibilities	Buyer's responsibilities
Cost, insurance and freight (CIF)	All export documentation and transportation costs and marine insurance against buyer's risk of loss to port of destination.	Likely will want additional marine insurance to supplement coverage provided by seller and assumes all costs and risk after ship arrives at port of destination.

From: **www.cbsc.org/alberta/tbl.cfm?fn=incoterm**

Use the following worksheet to calculate a CIF price. This calculation will give you the price of an export delivered to the buyer's port. The buyer covers all costs and risk after the ship arrives at the destination port.

---

[8]   A good discussion on CIF export costing is in: FITTskills, *International Marketing Entry and Distribution: Participant's Manual*, (Ottawa: Forum for International Trade Training, revised 2002), pp.61-79.

Figure 11: Export costing worksheet (CIF)

Category	Detailed Items	Costs	Timing
Marketing and promotion	▪ Agent's and distributor's fees ▪ Advertising ▪ Travel ▪ Communications ▪ Trade fairs and exhibits		
Production	▪ Unit cost of manufacture ▪ Product modification ▪ (Note: the profit margin should have been included by this time)		
Preparation	▪ Labelling ▪ Packaging ▪ Packing ▪ Marking		
Documentation	▪ Inspection ▪ Certification ▪ Preparation of documents ▪ Marine (Cargo) insurance ▪ Freight forwarder's fees		
Transportation	▪ Ocean freight (lading and related charges) ▪ Trucking (carriage) ▪ Warehousing and storage ▪ Insurance		
Financing	▪ Costs of financing documents ▪ Interest charges ▪ Exchange rate fluctuations ▪ Export credit insurance		

In value-based pricing, this emphasis is reversed and consideration of costs follows a consideration of what the market is prepared to pay.

Determining the export price starts with precise export costing calculations. They can be facilitated with the use of an export-costing sheet such as the one below proposed by ExportSource. Figure 12, is not for CIF price calculations but for calculating a price for goods that are landed in the target market – DDP or delivered duty paid.

Incoterms™2000	Seller's responsibilities	Buyer's responsibilities
Delivered duty paid (DDP)	*Maximum responsibility* for seller; all costs and risks to a specific destination in the importing country (includes costs such as unloading fees, storage, import license, fees, duties and taxes, custom broker's fees, ground transport, loading and unloading fees, insurance, etc.)	*Minimum responsibility* and risk to buyer; all costs and risks covered by seller until buyer actually receives the goods Exporter has to handle any customs clearance problems

Source: **www.cbsc.org/alberta/tbl.cfm?fn=incoterm**

Figure 12: Export costing worksheet (DDP)

Category	Detailed Items	Costs	Timing
Marketing and promotion	<ul><li>Agent's and distributor's fees</li><li>Advertising</li><li>Travel</li><li>Communications</li><li>Trade fairs and exhibits</li></ul>		
Production	<ul><li>Unit cost of manufacture</li><li>Product modification</li><li>(Note: the profit margin should have been included by this time)</li></ul>		
Preparation	<ul><li>Labelling</li><li>Packaging</li><li>Packing</li><li>Marking</li></ul>		
Documentation	<ul><li>Inspection</li><li>Certification</li><li>Preparation of documents</li><li>Marine (Cargo) insurance</li><li>Freight forwarder's fees</li></ul>		

Category	Detailed Items	Costs	Timing
Transportation	▪ Ocean freight (lading and related charges) ▪ Trucking (carriage) ▪ Warehousing and storage ▪ Insurance		

Profit margins

It is assumed in the previous example that the profit margin is included in the EXWorks price. However there are many ways to calculate the profit margin. Some companies calculate the profit on the EXWorks cost, some at a point midway in the calculations and some calculate the profit margin on the final cost, which then gives them their final price.

It may turn out that the price the company needs to cover its specified costs and provide an adequate profit margin is higher than the prices of competing offerings available in the target market. If that is so, the company has several alternatives:

- It can decide not to export the product to that market.

- It can try to reduce costs, by offering a stripped-down version of the product and incorporating less expensive materials, as long as the design change costs do not offset these cost savings. (For example, automotive companies, when shipping to hot climates, often don't include heaters in the cars. They may offer stripped down versions of the cars to keep the price lower).

- The company can try to reduce the mark-ups to the end-users along the distribution channel, by reducing its own margin or negotiating lower commissions. It may even shorten the channel, by adopting the activities of a channel member, if it believes it could carry out those activities more efficiently itself. The firm may also want to look at different modes of market entry, such as foreign manufacturing, assembly or licensing.

- The company can consider positioning the product as a premium product, by stressing the appeal of non-price features such as packaging, reliability of supply, speed of delivery, continuous innovation and after-sales service.

9.4 Highlights

- **Pricing varies depending on the market objectives being pursued.**

- **The factors influencing pricing strategy are directly linked to a company's marketing strategy.**

Case questions for discussion

1. When Mondetta is asked to quote on a container load of sportswear, how should they quote? EXW, CIF or DDP?

2. Before setting their international prices, should Mondetta check the retail (wholesale) prices in the target market? How would they do this?

3. Has your firm calculated their export prices? How did they do this?

10. International Marketing of Services

Objectives

The objectives for this chapter are as follows:

- **Explain the growth of and potential for the exporting of services abroad.**

- **Outline the challenges that a company may encounter in marketing services internationally.**

- **Identify customer needs that must be addressed when developing the marketing strategy for services.**

10.1 The growth of trade in services

Industrialized nations are evolving into service economies. The service sector in Canada, and indeed the world, is growing at a phenomenal rate. Because of Canada's past emphasis on raw materials and manufacturing, most marketing techniques have traditionally been geared to selling products rather than services.

The export of services is a new wave set to change the face of the Canadian economy. Canada's fortunes are rooted in the country's history and geography. Canadians have become experts in developing the complex and sophisticated systems of resource exploitation, telecommunications, transportation and engineering which have tied the country together. This expertise will lead to the next export boom, which will focus on international selling of this country's expertise in all of these areas.

The rapid growth of trade in services is symptomatic of the emphasis placed on knowledge and know-how in today's international economy. Not all services, however, are easily exported. Most personal services (e.g. personal grooming, housekeeping, home care and maintenance) are traded virtually, exclusively on the domestic market. Many other types of services, especially those provided to businesses (consulting, accounting, forwarding) can be more readily exported. And certain types of services around large capital projects (engineering, project management, design) have been a mainstay of the international trade in services for decades.

Service trade can take place in several different ways. When a deliverable service is produced in one country and transported to another, the service trade transaction is very similar to a merchandise trade transaction. For example, a client in one country can order data-processing services from another. The work is done in the supplier country and then sent electronically to the purchaser.

Service trade transactions can also be quite different, requiring either the buyer or the seller to cross a national boundary so the service can be provided. This may be the case, for example, if a supplier is contracted to manage a construction project in another country.

The movement of products, passengers or communications signals may in itself constitute a service. This would be the case if people were taken from one country to another for training, or if the training were provided electronically (e.g. over the Internet).

Some transactions, relating to rights to use intellectual property (e.g. licensing), are more intangible. In other cases, services are embodied in goods, sold together with products as an export package, or applied domestically to foreign products (e.g. maintenance, testing and repair services).

Since many services are intangible and highly "perishable" (i.e. time-sensitive, for example, magazines, newspapers), they can be delivered to foreign customers only by establishing a presence in the market. This presence may be either temporary or permanent, involving foreign direct investment. In some cases, the delivery of services to foreign clients may involve both an investment in a foreign operation and the export of services from home. Some service exports arise through providing services to the foreign operations themselves.

International trade in services is growing more quickly than traditional trade in the resource-based and manufacturing sectors. The established transportation and tourism sectors account for part of the rapid growth in commercial services trade. But the fastest growing and now single most important component is other private services, such as medical care, accounting, management consulting, project management, engineering and various types of financial services.

> *"With regard to the direction of Canada's trade in services, the United States remains Canada's principal trading partner. The share of the United States in Canada's two-way trade is smaller for services (59.4 percent) than for merchandise (79.4 percent). The United States is becoming an increasingly important market, accounting for 57.7 percent of Canada's services exports in 2001, compared to 56.8 percent in 1989. Turning to imports, the US share fell from 62.5 percent in 1989 to 60.8 percent in 2001."*

Source: **www.itcan.gc.ca**

Similarly, business or producer services account for the largest part of Canada's exports of commercial services and represent the area with the greatest export potential for Canada. Unlike goods exports, which are heavily focused toward the US, Canada's services exports are more geographically-diversified. While 87 percent of all goods are exported to the US, only 60 percent of service receipts come from the US. About 7 percent of our goods are shipped to Asia compared with 10 percent of our services. Finally, Europe is the destination for 5 percent of goods but 20 percent of our services.

Figure 13: Destinations of Canadian exports by market in 2000 (percent)

Country	Goods	Services
US	87	60
Asia (incl. Japan)	7	10
Europe	5	20
Other	1	10

Source: **www.edc.ca/docs/ereports/speeches/2004/Economics/WTS_e.pdf**, pp. 7 - 8.

Producer services include the service categories listed in the following figure.

Figure 14: Examples of producer services

Accounting	Health care services
Architectural services	Industrial design
Communications services	Legal services
Computer services	Management consulting
Construction services	Personnel services
Consulting engineering	Scientific services
Distribution (retail and wholesale) services	Security services
Environmental services	Training services
Financial services	Transportation and logistics services
Geomatic services	

For additional information, tips and tools on the subject of trade in services and its importance for Canada, go to *Take a World View, Export Your Services* at:

www.exportsource.ca/worldview

For information and data on world trade in services, go to *World Trade Organization, Trade Topics, Services* at:

www.wto.org

For a discussion paper on services in the new economy go to:

www.strategis.ic.gc.ca/epic/internet/ineas-aes.nsf/vwapj/dp13e.pdf/$FILE/dp13e.pdf

10.2 The challenge of marketing services internationally

Difficult as it is to sell tangible products in a foreign country, it is even harder to sell services. The intangibility of services makes differentiating and demonstrating "value-added" more difficult.

Service exporters are marketing a "promise to deliver" rather than a concrete product that one can touch and feel. In effect, they are selling the value of their experience and credibility. When this is combined with the cultural and communication problems normally faced in international business, the selling of services abroad can become very challenging.

Communicating the service being offered is particularly difficult. As a rule, the service provider cannot hand out samples, and even brochures tend to be limited to showing a "proxy" for the service (e.g. a picture of a completed building conveys more about the performance of construction services than a picture of a construction site). Considerable effort is required to translate the intangibility of a service into a tangible and saleable offer.

Services are difficult to standardize and often must be tailored to specific client needs. This need for adaptation frequently gives rise to requirements for direct client participation and cooperation in the delivery of services.

With direct customer involvement often required, and the major asset of service firms frequently being the knowledge of the principals involved, personal selling plays a particularly important role in marketing services. Marketing services abroad requires more personal networking and face-to-face selling time than for products, and thus adds to the overall marketing expense.

Marketing services also implies establishing friendship and trust; this takes much more time in foreign markets than at home. Therefore, understanding the particular local environment of the market, including its culture and politics, is very important.

Services usually imply a substantial degree of local involvement; therefore, the company planning to market services abroad needs to consider the following environmental factors:

- language;

- education and levels of skill;

- attitudes toward service tasks;

- legislation concerning the employment of local people;

- male and female roles in society;

- working conditions (e.g. hours of work);

- motivational techniques which differ from country to country; and

- pay equity.

In exporting services, people issues are not the only important consideration. Access to communications networks and the capability to move data can be critical to providing knowledge-intensive services.

Often, a commercial presence must be established abroad to provide the necessary proximity to customers, the feel for the market and to signify the company's standing in the market. This presence, too, adds to the costs of marketing services internationally. Lead times to develop sales can be extensive. And once the work is secured, service business managers face the challenge of juggling requirements to do the work with the search for future contracts.

Services are also distinguished, in many cases, by their time dependency. Service firms are particularly sensitive to timeliness in market information. A service can often be offered only at a specific time, otherwise it loses relevance. Trying to provide a service from a domestic base of operations, while adhering to domestic hours of operation, may not satisfy customers located half way around the world.

Service firms can find financing difficult, in part because they often lack the hard assets necessary to meet lending requirements. Because services are intangible, the normal procedures and securities used in exporting goods do not apply. Furthermore, setting a value on services or establishing when the terms of a contract have been fulfilled can be more difficult than for product exports. As a result, disputes over payment are also more difficult to assess.

Service exports can also face some distinctive obstacles to market access. In general, these obstacles relate to the following:

- professional qualifications (e.g. requirements for accreditation, constraints on the exercise of a profession) and the mobility of personnel (e.g. visas, work permits);

- types of cross-border service transactions, methods of market entry (including ownership restrictions), conditions for operations and competition;

- inadequate protection for intellectual property;

- discriminatory host country procurement practices;

- public assistance to local firms (to compete in domestic or export markets) and the role of state-owned enterprise;

- international payments (e.g. restrictions on repatriation of profits, fees, royalties) and discriminatory taxation; and

- technical impediments (e.g. in standards, network access restrictions, constraints on technology and information transfers).

Notwithstanding these challenges, it is generally agreed that internationally-active service firms can typically enter foreign markets then much smaller than typical first-time merchandise exporters. Moreover, smaller service firms can be just as active as larger ones in foreign markets.

10.3 Choosing a marketing strategy for services

The key to successful marketing of services is to develop marketing strategies around the needs of the target customers. This requires developing an understanding of those customers' needs and desires, as well as what factors they consider to be important to their purchasing decisions.

The marketer offering services will find the following factors important:

- the perception that the provider of the service has past experience applicable to the situation at hand;

- factors that make the service or the supplier stand out (e.g. differentiating along the lines of more "brains" or talent);

- superior procedures and methods (e.g. better offices and facilities);

- a positive corporate image (e.g. successful, equipped with good references);

- an effective personal "sales pitch"; and

- service costs.

In purchasing services, buyers frequently place confidence in the supplier ahead of cost considerations. Image can help build that confidence. Where services are highly intangible and complex, prospective clients often seek out and assess "surrogate" indicators of service quality – office decor and cleanliness, the look of brochures, and the appearance, demeanor and communications skills of staff. Thus, a vital sub-task in understanding the customer's purchase decision is finding out what aspects of image matter in the target markets.

Taking these considerations into account, the exporter offering services can then work toward achieving its primary objective; namely, positioning itself as a recognizable supplier in the foreign market. Such a supplier is one who is an acknowledged expert, has a good reputation for its business dealings and is able to offer services effectively. Achieving this requires the development of marketing strategies focused on getting exposure and management of client expectations.

10.4 Promoting services in international markets

In marketing services, getting exposure is likely to be best achieved by targeted approaches, often involving personal contacts. Networking with a company's own customers can be a particularly effective avenue for gaining exposure.

Clients, past and present, can greatly strengthen the service supplier's credibility, by providing references and supplying comments suitable for quotation in the company's sales literature. Satisfied customers, along with professional colleagues, can be excellent sources of referrals.

These referrals should be requested and cultivated with gratitude and reciprocal gestures. It is said that if a service company can attain a 35 percent referral rate, they will be successful in the near and long term. Clients may also be able to provide introductions to other potential customers in the target market.

Using the media effectively, particularly foreign trade publications, can also be critical. Companies must learn not just to advertise, but to cultivate media relationships to obtain additional, favourable publicity about themselves and their services.

Raising the company's profile through speaking engagements at industry and professional functions and participating in trade shows and conventions can also bring good results. Direct mail and telemarketing approaches also have their place.

At all times, the company needs to tailor its message to the contact being made, recognizing the contact's particular priorities and the benefit the service supplier hopes to achieve from making the contact. All marketing tools (e.g. business cards, brochures, customer lists, summaries of prior experience, testimonials, media pieces, videos and diskettes) convey an impression of the company and must be of top quality to project the desired image. All contacts represent an opportunity for the supplier to emphasize its uniqueness.

Sales promotions can help convey this impression. Among the promotions used by service marketers are free- or low-rate trials, free initial consultations, free access to supporting services and free seminars or publications. Service guarantees can also be used to set the company apart from its competitors.

Planning the personal sales effort deserves particular attention. The company needs to consider whether, and to what degree, billable staff time should be tied up in selling, whether the firm could afford dedicated sales efforts, and whether agents could be relied upon to have sufficient technical expertise and motivation to sustain a sales effort.

Sometimes an international trade project will require services as part of a larger contract. Best known at home for building the widely acclaimed Terminal 3 at Toronto's Pearson International Airport, Canada's Airport Development Corporation's (ADC) has recently completed a terminal project worth $140 million at Budapest's Ferihegy International Airport. The services ADC provided in that project included:

- performance of a thorough assessment, to ensure that the commercial risks could be fully absorbed by all the private-sector participants;

- arranging that the Royal Bank of Canada led the financing of the project. The syndicated loan was oversubscribed.

Source: **www.ccc.ca/eng/suc_airport.cfm**

In other projects, a consortium led by Airport Development Corporation has been awarded a 35-year concession to finance, design, construct and operate the new US$ 550 million international airport in Quito, Ecuador as well as to operate the existing Mariscal Sucre Airport in Quito while the new airport is being constructed. For additional information about ADC, see:

Source: **www.adccanada.com/quito.html**

10.5 Highlights

- International trade in services is growing at a faster rate than the trade in goods.

- Service exporters are marketing a "promise to deliver" rather than concrete product which one can touch and feel.

- The key to successful marketing of services is to develop marketing strategies around the needs of the customers.

Case questions for discussion

1. Does Mondetta have any services which they could sell abroad?

2. Should they be considering a market strategy for services?

3. Does your firm have any marketable services?

4. Are you exporting services now? Any plans for the future?

Appendix 1: Case Study

Mondetta Clothing of Winnipeg

Note: This case study is based on a series of articles, cases, and press releases from over the past decade as well as conversations in 2004 with senior management.

Articles

Entrepreneurship – Capturing the Spirit (Condensed)
Crystal Jorgenson, Career Planning and Placement Service
University of Manitoba, November 3, 1993

"Ash Modha, president and partner of the Winnipeg company Mondetta, considers passion vital to entrepreneurship. What is required, he says, is "the passion to take something from nothing and make it something, take it from an embryonic stage and sustain it."

Mondetta, which means "small world", began as a promotional goods business in 1987. Modha and his partners set up shop on the beach, selling T-shirts and sweatshirts to the university crowd. But something was missing; sales were terrible and competition was tough.

"Awareness" was the key, said Modha. The next weekend, Mondetta sponsored a skateboard team demonstration. "They were really lousy," he admitted, however, several hundred people gathered to watch and Mondetta sold $10,000 worth of product that weekend.

Modha and his partners progressed from direct retail to agent distribution, starting in western Canada. They developed their uniquely embroidered sweatshirts, which, despite an initial skeptical reaction from retailers, met with huge success.

Expansion is a primary concern in the clothing business. "We have to open up new markets," said Modha. "Now we've come to a point where we've sustained the business, we're growing, but we're not doing it in the territories where we started."

Mondetta, now with distribution in the United States, Japan, and Italy, has challenged the myth that Canadians are not internationally competitive. "If you have a good product, you can sell it anywhere. We're starting to ship Canadian products – made in Winnipeg, Manitoba, Canada – to Italy, the fashion capital of the world," said Modha.

Modha admitted that the entrepreneur lives in constant fear of going broke or losing out to the competition. Nevertheless, he believes "the more scared you are, the harder you try."

Forge a Strong Export Team Abroad and at Home
Trade Stories, *Exporting Canada Online*
Friday, January 23, 1998

"WHOEVER THOUGHT a Winnipeg clothing company, with an Italian name, would be selling fashion to Italy?" wonders Ash Modha, 28-year-old president of Mondetta Clothing. Apart from Italy, Mondetta is selling its high-end sportswear in a dozen other countries. Exports now account for about 10 percent of the company's annual revenues of $10 million. All that will change next year when the company hires its first export manager – it's looking to triple export revenues over the next three years.

The company's strategy is to organize its diverse distribution arrangements with agents and middlemen worldwide to create an organized alliance of about 20 offshore distributors who will concentrate on sales and market development. Home base will look after manufacturing and shipping.

In five years, Modha hopes to be opening offices overseas, but he cautions would-be exporters to be patient in finding market niches. The offshore distributors a company links up with often don't start turning in huge sales overnight – it's usually necessary to wait up to three years to get a viable business up and running in a foreign country. The clothing business presents unique challenges for exporters, adds Prashant Modha, Ash's 30-year-old brother and Mondetta's vice-president of finance. The process is intensely administrative, involving quotas, export licenses and complex customs and commercial documentation. "Start small," he advises new exporters. "The paperwork for your first one-container shipment will always be wrong – but by the time you're shipping 10 containers, you'll get the hang of it."

One of the trickiest areas for exporters, says Prashant, is letters of credit, which are routinely used by foreign customers to pay for goods. Normally, Mondetta won't start production on an order until a workable letter of credit is in place. A confirmed letter of credit guarantees payment for the goods as long as the terms of the credit are met. A good letter of credit can be given to suppliers or used as security for a loan, and Prashant advises, "forming a close relationship" with a bank that is experienced in trade financing. "This is not something that they can usually handle at the local branch level," he says. "It's very tricky and needs expert knowledge and advice."

For example, sometimes a letter of credit demands that invoice documentation must be in triplicate original form and signed in blue ink so there can be no risk of photocopies. Make sure it's done, says Prashant.

An exporter must also watch out for "goofy conditions" he says, terms which make the contract difficult or impossible to perform. Sometimes the letter of credit will provide for shipment on a specific ship on a specific date, which may not allow you to adequately complete the complex paperwork.

An exporter should refuse to accept such a letter and ask the purchaser for an amendment. The bank, says Prashant, will usually catch a variation of standard letter of credit terms, but they won't always know about things like shipping schedules – that is the exporter's responsibility.

If paperwork isn't done properly, an exporter may not get paid after delivering the goods, or the customer may refuse to accept them when they arrive at the dock. Practically, that usually means the exporter has to offer a "big discount" to get the customer to sign off on the deal.

All that said, this is a good time to jump into exporting, says Prashant, because World Trade Organization rules are slowly eliminating import quotas (with some countries abolishing them entirely) and tariffs and duties are also on the way down."

'Fine-tuned' Mondetta set to sign $1.3-M pact Transformed firm adapts to changing market (Condensed)
Geoff Kirbyson, *Winnipeg Free Press*
Friday, March 1, 2002

"With a $1.3-million contract about to be signed, Ash Modha says there is little doubt the transformation of Mondetta Clothing Inc. is complete."

Gone are the days when the Winnipeg-based clothier would ship a few dozen of its marquee item -- sweatshirts emblazoned with flags from around the world -- to any mom and pop store that would take them.

Today, the Winnipeg-based clothier has narrowed its retail focus to a select few stores that will carry a significant amount of its product. Its production is now driven around higher quality fabric and more intricate designs and the company has complemented its retail business by branching out to add corporate and private label divisions.

"Mondetta has been reinvented, or fine-tuned, in the last year or two," Modha said in an interview.

"The whole landscape is completely different from when we started in retail (back in 1990). We've had to completely change our business to (adapt) to changing market conditions."

As a private company, Mondetta isn't required to disclose financial figures, but Modha did say its retail business, representing about 60 percent of its total, has doubled in the last year, while its corporate division has grown 50 percent over the same period. Its one-year-old private label business is on pace to generate more than $1 million in revenues this year, he added.

The "fine-tuning" has resulted in Mondetta increasing its employee base to 32, up from 16 in 1998.

Modha said his employees find the three-year-old corporate division the most enjoyable.

"That's where our design and creative departments have so much fun. We'll sit down with the customer and design a whole program from scratch for them. We don't buy goods from a distributor and drop a logo on it," he said.

Mondetta designs products such as sweatshirts, T-shirts, golf shirts, leather goods and golf bags for corporate customers that include Sony, BMW, the American Ballet Theater, Circle du Soleil, as well as local firms such as Palliser Furniture and the Winnipeg Airports Authority.

Modha said the $1.3-million deal with a national firm will be finalized soon. With contract sizes starting at a minimum of about $15,000, the attraction to this side of the business is obvious, he said.

Mondetta produces the Mondetta Air clothing line, featuring T-shirts, hats and jackets, exclusively for the WAA (Winnipeg Airports Authority). The items are either used for promotion or sold in the Showcase Manitoba store in the terminal building.

"We formed a partnership with Mondetta Clothing to produce our promotional and sponsorship products, including Mondetta Air, as they are a Manitoba company producing world-class products," said Lyn Book, director of corporate communications for the WAA.

Mondetta's private label business serves retailers such as Galyans, a US-based lifestyle store similar to Mountain Equipment Co-op, as well as Canadian clothing outlets such as Bootlegger, which want to offer their own branded clothing to customers. Mondetta will then design, develop and ship product to the retailer, emblazoned with its individual logo.

"Many of the big retailers lack the design capabilities and the ability to bring quality products into their stores. We can bridge the gap for them and they get Mondetta quality and design," he said.

James Umlah, chief investment officer of Crocus Investment Fund, which has more than $800,000 invested in Mondetta, said he was impressed with the way Modha and his team, including Prashant Modha, its CFO, and vice-president of sales Raj Bahl have modified their position in the marketplace to meet changing demands."

Telephone conversations

During phone calls in 2004, Prashant Modha, Vice President of Finance provided the following information.

Mondetta's first central marketing principal was to give people a product they wanted to buy, even if at first they didn't know they wanted to buy it. Mondetta says they did this by providing a much better product than was currently available, T-shirts, sweatshirts and other items with very high quality embroidery. The company felt that when the customers examined the product, they would recognize the quality and "would just have to buy it." This strategy worked.

Mondetta, after initial overseas development, wanted to expand, but was flexible in its approach. Mondetta had an ad hoc and very flexible international marketing plan.

They tested different markets, mostly in Europe. Mondetta's foray into Italy came through a trade show in the US An Italian distributor approached them and the two companies developed an agreement for the Italian distributor to handle Mondetta's products in Italy. The Italian distributor already had a line of shoes, the family owners wanted a line of clothing and Mondetta's product was very attractive. The Italian distributor was realistic and they were successful in that market.

They indirectly exported to Japan through a Vancouver based trading company who approached them with an order. All other exports, mainly to Europe were done directly to distributors in the various target markets.

Cultural differences mean different things to different people. Mondetta's biggest challenge was that they were not well known outside of Canada as their competitors, i.e. Tommy Hilfiger, in the global market.

They had some difficulties initially in the US market – they didn't understand it. So they made an agreement with a Canadian distributor, who had been successful in the UK market with their products, to handle the US market, but that distributor was also unsuccessful, as they didn't know how to sell in the US market.

For the US and Italy, as well as the rest of Europe, Canadian sizes seemed to fit well into the market. However for Japan and the rest of East Asia, everything had to be smaller.

Mondetta does sell services, but they are wrapped up with the product. Because of their international experience, Mondetta has very good import as well as export contacts and experience. Using these contacts and expertise, Mondetta will source product offshore, for Canadian clothing manufacturers. For some private label business, they will design the product and then show the customer how to sell the finished product.

Epilogue

In 1998, Mondetta had been very optimistic about export markets, but reality began to set in. The company realized that their export markets were fragmented and were not as profitable as previously expected; Mondetta did not hire an export manager in 1999 as the articles suggested and they did not open overseas sales offices. However, ironically they did open some buying offices overseas. Prashant says that his comments, in the 1998 case, on trade finance, letters of credit still stand.

At this point, 2004, Mondetta is no longer involved in European, US, Japanese or Korean markets. They have become more focused on major retailers in Canada who are prepared to make volume orders and pay on a regular basis. Mondetta is also manufacturing for private labels. There were various difficulties marketing to "mom & pop" operations, including payment issues and they no longer target this market.

Looking ahead for exporting, in two years time, Mondetta hopes to be in either China or India. They have determined that both countries have a rapidly growing middle class. These two groups targeted have the disposable income to buy Mondetta's clothing/fashion products.

Case revised, consolidated by D.H. Wallace, July, 2004.

Appendix 2: Case Study Answers

Chapter 1

1. **Which of the key principles discussed in this chapter has Mondetta followed in its approach?**

   Mondetta's first central marketing principle was to give people a product they wanted to buy, even if at first they didn't know they wanted to buy it. Mondetta says they did this by providing a much better product than was currently available – T-shirts, sweatshirts and other items with very high quality embroidery. The company felt that when the customers examined the product, they would recognize the quality and "would just have to buy it." This strategy worked.

Chapter 2

1. **Is Mondetta's international marketing approach different from their domestic approach? Explain how.**

   Mondetta's foray into Italy came through a trade show in the US. An Italian distributor approached them and the two companies developed an agreement for the Italian distributor to handle Mondetta's products in Italy.

Chapter 3

1. **What information from the articles would lead us to conclude that Mondetta has an international marketing plan?**

   Mondetta had an ad hoc and very flexible international marketing plan. They tested different markets, mostly in Europe. The Italian distributor already had a line of shoes, the family owners wanted a line of clothing and Mondetta's product was very attractive.

Chapter 4

1. **In what situation should Mondetta consider direct marketing? Indirect marketing?**

   After initial overseas development, Mondetta wanted to expand, but was flexible in its approach. They indirectly exported to Japan through a Vancouver-based trading company which approached them with an order. All other exports, mainly to Europe were done directly to distributors in the various target markets. If Mondetta is approached by a Canadian trading company in Canada, with an order for a market in which they are not yet involved, they might consider an indirect export through the trading company. They should export directly into any market that they know and in which they have good and reliable distributor contacts.

2. **If Mondetta has an exclusive agent in Italy, and the Canadian subsidiary of an Italian company wants to buy from Mondetta on an EXWorks basis, what should Mondetta do?**

Mondetta should, and is probably legally required to, refer the potential buyer to their Italian distributor.

3. **What is Mondetta's niche? What did they do to develop this niche?**

Mondetta's niche is high quality, fashionable, casual clothes with good quality printing. They first developed this niche by trial and error; people were looking for a high quality product that Mondetta found they could supply.

Chapter 5

1. **Can you identify the cultural differences that Mondetta has faced as they have entered each new market?**

Cultural differences mean different things to different people. Mondetta's biggest challenge was that they were not as well known outside of Canada as their competitors, i.e. Tommy Hilfiger, in the global market.

2. **If they expand into other international markets, will they face other differences?**

They plan to be either in India (which they think they know) or in China (which they know they don't know).

Chapter 6

1. **What sort of rules and regulations will Mondetta face when operating in the US, Europe or Asia?**

Discuss American regulation, transport and commerce. Also ask participants for stories of the company's experience in the US, Europe or Asia.

2. **When operating in the US, will Mondetta face different regulations than in Canada?**

A good place to start is US immigration and how it affects Canadians doing business in the US.

Chapter 7

1. **Do we know if Mondetta has modified its sizes and styles for offshore markets?**

   For the US and Italy, as well as the rest of Europe, Canadian sizes seemed to fit well into the market. However for Japan and the rest of East Asia, everything had to be smaller.

2. **What strategies should they adopt to do the above?**

   Talk to your customers and distributors. Manufacturers of blue Jeans had to learn this lesson when they first entered the Japanese market: Jeans had to be resized. They learned this from clothing distributors and consumers. Japanese body shapes are different. Kitchen-cabinet manufactures also face the same challenge. They learned this from Japanese construction people and cabinet manufacturers.

Chapter 8

1. **If Mondetta is planning to exhibit at a trade show in Milan, what languages should their literature be in?**

   If their current cards are in English – then English and Italian. If their cards are bilingual English and French, then English and French one side and Italian on the other. Some part of the card should definitely be in Italian.

2. **Should the Mondetta representatives' business cards be in several languages – if so which ones?**

   Normally when doing business in Winnipeg, Mondetta business cards should be in English. However, cards in English and French, depending on where they do business in Canada, might be a good idea.

Chapter 9

1. **When Mondetta is asked to quote on a container load of sportswear, how should they quote? EXW, CIF or DDP?**

   Normally a company would quote on a CIF basis, but it depends on what the customer wants. In some countries e.g. Japan, the customer may have access to very low insurance rates and therefore will request a CFR (C&F) quote. In some landlocked European countries, the customer may request a quote delivered directly to their warehouse.

2. **Before setting their international prices, should Mondetta check the retail (wholesale) prices in the target market? How would they do this?**

   Talk to their potential distributors, ask for assistance from Canadian trade commissioners in the target market and/or make a market visit to the target market.

Chapter 10

1. Does Mondetta have any services which they could sell abroad?

Mondetta does sell services, but they are wrapped up with the product. Because of their international experience, Mondetta has very good import as well as export contacts and experience. Using these contacts and expertise, Mondetta will source offshore product for Canadian clothing manufacturers. For some private label business, they will design the product and then show the customer how to sell the finished product.

2. Should they be considering a market strategy for services?

Their current strategy seems to be working. However, they should review this from time to time to see if they can improve their business in services.

Appendix 3: International Marketing Plan Template

1. What business are you in?	
Provide a brief description of your business	
What added value do you offer your customers?	
What is unique about your business? Why would customers come to you as opposed to going elsewhere?	
2. Why export?	
Why do you want to export?	
How important a role do you want exporting to play in your business?	
What market do you think would be able to support this role for your firm? Why?	

3. Sources of information	
What published materials are available on your target market: • Internet sites • periodicals • books • country reports • sectoral profiles • specialized studies • other?	
Which of the following can provide information about the target market: • ITCan country desk • foreign embassy in Canada • Canadian trade commissioner in the target market • companies doing business in the target market • business intermediaries in Canada or in the target country?	
Are any special facilities available: • federal programs, especially any focused on the target market • provincial programs focused on the target market • Canadian business councils focused on the target country?	
What are your best sources of secondary information? How complete and reliable are they?	
Will it be possible or feasible to conduct any primary market research in the target country? If so, what are the impediments to performing this research? How do you propose to overcome them?	

4. The target market	
Size and dynamics	
How big is the existing market for your product or service (or similar products or services) in the target country in terms of: ▪ value per year ▪ volume (units sold) ▪ number of customers?	
Over the past 5 to 10 years has this market been: ▪ growing ▪ staying even ▪ shrinking	
What proportion of this market is supplied by imports from another country: ▪ in value per year ▪ in volume?	
Over the past 5 to 10 years, have imports (in your product or service area, or one similar to it) been: ▪ rising ▪ staying even ▪ falling (in absolute terms and as a percentage of the total market)?	
Competitors	
Who are the most significant domestic (in-country) suppliers of the product or service (or similar products or services) in terms of: ▪ absolute value/volume ▪ market share?	
How do they compare with your firm in terms of: ▪ size ▪ capacity ▪ assets and strengths?	

Who are the most significant foreign (importing) suppliers of the product or service (or similar products or services) in terms of: ■ absolute value/volume ■ market share?	
How do they compare with your firm in terms of: ■ size ■ capacity ■ assets and strengths?	
Customers	
Who buys the product or service (or similar ones) that you propose to export: ■ end-users (consumers) ■ businesses ■ governments ■ other?	
What do you know or can you find out about the characteristics of the buyers in terms of: ■ why they buy ■ how much they buy ■ where and how they buy?	
What do your buyers care most about? ■ price ■ quality ■ functionality ■ design ■ prestige ■ safety or security ■ timeliness ■ reliability ■ other?	

What factors might affect the decision to buy: • fashion • social consciousness • level of development • level of technological development • business climate • political attitudes (e.g. toward foreigners) • other?	
Does the country have significant cultural or social characteristics that might influence the buying decision: • religion • social taboos • cultural preferences • habits and customs • ethical considerations • other?	
Market objectives	
Given why you want to export and the role you want exporting to play in your company, what role will this market play in your company's plans? How does this compare with other markets to which you are exporting or want to export?	
What share of the target market do you need to capture to achieve these objectives?	
Pricing strategy	
At what price(s) is the product/service currently offered in the target market?	
What factors influence prices in the target market? Is the market price sensitive? Can you correlate changes in prices to changes in demand?	

Are there any restrictions on your ability to set a price?	
At what price could you offer your product or service and still make a profit? Factor in your costs, expected margins and the impact of different sales volumes.	
Given what you know of price sensitivity in the target market and your own cost structure, what percentage of the market could you credibly hope to address on the basis of price alone (and still make a profit)?	
How does this compare with your stated objectives in the market?	

5. The product

Are products or services similar to your own already offered in the target market? How does what is available compare to yours in terms of: ▪ quality ▪ functionality ▪ design ▪ prestige ▪ safety or security ▪ ease of assembly or maintenance ▪ other?	
How would you have to modify your product or service to enhance its appeal to customers?	

Would the customers' perceived value of the product or service increase significantly if you were able to offer: ▪ timely or reliable delivery ▪ delivery to locations other than those normal in the target country ▪ a different way of selling the product ▪ unique positioning (i.e. as a luxury import) ▪ other?	
6. Market entry	
Political environment	
Are there any political impediments to selling the product or service: ▪ instability ▪ discriminatory treatment of foreigners ▪ protectionism ▪ restrictions on trade or investment ▪ other?	
Are there any Canadian restrictions on controls or exporting to the target country?	
Business environment	
Are there fiscal impediments: ▪ currency controls ▪ high tariffs ▪ repatriation of profits ▪ limits on investment ▪ tax rates or double taxation ▪ other?	

Is the business infrastructure adequate to support the proposed venture in terms of: ▪ banking ▪ insurance ▪ credit checks on partners and clients ▪ accounting practices ▪ other business services?	
Does business law in the target country offer adequate protection for property, including intellectual property? Is it adequate in terms of dispute resolution?	
Is the physical infrastructure sufficient to support the proposed venture in terms of transportation, warehousing/storage and telecommunications?	
What, if any, is the impact of geography or climate on the proposed venture?	
Entry strategy	
Does the company already possess a ready, reputable and reliable facility to manufacture, package and ship the product to market?	
What are the existing channels of distribution available and the costs associated with each step in the chain?	
Is the target market normally served through direct sales, distributors or agents?	
Is loss of control over marketing in the foreign market going to be an issue if a foreign agent or distributor is used?	

What market entry alternatives are available in terms of: ▪ trading houses ▪ co-production agreements ▪ co-marketing arrangements ▪ joint ventures ▪ franchises ▪ license agreements ▪ direct investment ▪ other?	
Are any significant advantages to be realized from any of these alternatives? What additional help/support is required: ▪ in-country legal, accounting or tax advisers ▪ intermediaries (in Canada or in the target market) ▪ research and development partners ▪ freight forwarders ▪ customs brokers ▪ investors ▪ other?	

7. Positioning and messages	
What does the target audience care about? How do you know? How can you find out more?	
What is unique about your product or service in the target market?	
What identity should the product or service have in the minds of its customers?	

What are the main messages that need to be conveyed about the product or service in terms of: ▪ quality ▪ price ▪ unique features ▪ prestige ▪ convenience ▪ other?	
How will the product or service be positioned vis-à-vis competing offerings?	
Are there established products, services or images that yours can be associated with? If so, what are they and how can the association be made?	
What local cultural or other characteristics have to be factored into the promotional message? What methods are currently being used to sell to the specific market in the target country?	
What marketing techniques are available for communicating with the target audience: ▪ personal visits and contacts ▪ trade missions ▪ trade fairs and exhibitions ▪ public launches and promotional events ▪ advertising (radio, television, print, outdoor) ▪ point-of-sale displays ▪ publications (magazines, newsletters) ▪ directories and catalogues ▪ Internet sites ▪ endorsements and testimonials through speeches or public events ▪ other? How feasible and/or appropriate is each of these methods to the product or service? What are the potential costs and benefits of each method?	

What techniques are appropriate and available to make the product or service more appealing to the target audience: - introductory offers - coupons - cross-marketing through established products or services - money-back guarantees - warranties for after-sales service - volume discounts - repeat sale discounts - other? What are the costs and benefits associated with each?	
8. Sales and distribution	
What customer concerns have to be satisfied when delivering the product or service to market: - timeliness - security and/or safety - reliability - delivery to a specific location - ambience at the point of purchase - other? How will these affect the marketing and sales effort?	
How is the product or service normally sold: - personal contact - general retail outlets - specialty stores - big-box discount stores - events - ordered through media - proposals and tenders - other?	

Is a local sales force required? If so, what qualifications does it need? How many people are required? What infrastructure does the sales force need?	
Is there a need for after-sales servicing? Can it be used to enhance promotion and marketing? Can it be used to generate follow-on business?	
What are the implications of providing local after-sales support in hiring and training of service personnel, stocking parts, infrastructure?	

9. Implementation

Who is responsible for overall implementation of the marketing plan? What kind of authority does this individual have to deploy all necessary resources?	
What kind of internal resources are available for the marketing effort in terms of: ■ senior executive commitment ■ funding ■ internal staff ■ other?	
What kind of marketing support does the firm need to enter the target market? What marketing support does it currently have in its domestic market? Is this support qualified in and suitable for the target market? Does it have any contacts with organizations in the target market?	
What local marketing support is available in the target market: ■ market research organizations ■ mail order houses ■ ad agencies ■ other?	

What promotional materials will be needed: • brochures • advertising copy • product descriptions and technical specifications • manuals for assembly and/or use • other? Who will prepare these (writing and design)? Will they need to be translated? Who will provide the translation? How much will it cost?	
How will sales be handled: • agent • distributor • hire local staff • send staff from Canada • local partner with a sales organization • other?	
What are the risks involved: • political risks • exchange-rate risks • business risks • market risks • other?	
What measures is the firm taking to reduce these risks? What measures are being taken to track client satisfaction?	
10. Monitor and measure	
How will the overall effort be monitored? What milestones and targets have been set? How will results be communicated to senior management at head office?	

Source: FITTskills, *International Marketing: Participant's Manual*, 2002.

Appendix 4: Sources of Assistance

There are numerous and diverse sources and types of assistance offered to entrepreneurs and exporters. We cannot list them all here. The following figure informs you of those considered to be of interest to most business people across the country.

Name and contact information	Type of assistance	Brief description
General information		
Team Canada Inc 1-888-811-1119	Team Canada Inc's toll-free export information service	Trained export information specialists help you to quickly access the right programs, services and resource people. Your call will be instantly directed to an information officer located in the Canada Business Service Centre in your province or territory. Hours of operation: 9 a.m. to 5 p.m., Monday to Friday.
ExportSource **www.exportsource.ca**	Team Canada Inc's online resource for export information	ExportSource is Canada's most comprehensive online source for export information. The site provides information on foreign markets, export financing, trade statistics, export contacts, trade shows and missions. There are guides on export preparation, business trip planning, trade show preparation, international project bids, and others.
Export Your Services: Take a World View **www.exportsource.ca/worldview**	Web site for exporters of services	Provides answers to frequently asked questions about exporting expertise, knowledge and skills. Features information on world markets for service exporters, available assistance and others.
Strategis **www.strategis.gc.ca**	Canada's largest business information web site	Canada's largest virtual library. Provides access to information on market trends, industry analyses, trade statistics and more.

Name and contact information	Type of assistance	Brief description
Skills development		
Forum for International Trade Training (FITT) Inc. 1-800-561-3488 **www.fitt.ca**	Developer of international trade training programs	The FITTskills program is delivered through colleges, universities and private training institutions across the country as well as online. FITT has introduced Canada's first professional designation in international trade, the Certified International Trade Professional (C.I.T.P.).
Market entry support		
The Canadian Trade Commissioner Service **www.infoexport.gc.ca**	Market preparation entry support	Advice and assistance for companies that are ready to enter foreign markets. The Canadian Trade Commissioner Service is staffed by trade commissioners, representing Industry Canada and International Trade Canada. They are your gateway to the Trade Commissioner Service abroad.
Canadian Commercial Corporation (CCC) 1-800-748-8191 **www.ccc.ca**	International trade facilitation	Contracting services, prime contractor in government-to-government contracts.
Trade financing		
Business Development Bank of Canada (BDC) 1-888-463-6232 **www.bdc.ca**	Financial and management services	Canada's small business bank. Focuses on emerging and exporting sectors.
Export Development Canada (EDC) 1-800-880-1884 **www.edc.ca**	Financial and risk management services	Canadian crown corporation providing export credit insurance, medium- and long-term financing and guarantees to support exporters.

Name and contact information	Type of assistance	Brief description
In-market services		
International Trade Canada (ITCan) **www.itcan-cican.gc.ca** Canadian Trade Commissioner Service **www.infoexport.gc.ca**	In-market assistance	International Trade Canada has a variety of programs and services to companies that are ready to enter foreign markets. One of the key services offered is the Trade Commissioner Service that helps companies that have researched and selected their target markets. Services offered include: Market Prospect, Key Contacts Search, Visit Information, Face-to-Face Briefing, Local Company Information, and Troubleshooting.

Appendix 5: Glossary

Accounts receivable turnover	A financial ratio calculated by dividing a firm's total sales by total accounts receivable, which shows how quickly accounts receivable can be collected, inventory sold and payment collected.
Advised letter of credit (L/C)	A bank document that informs the exporter that a L/C has been established in favour of the exporter by the importer.
Advising bank	A financial institution that is the intermediary between the beneficiary (exporter) and the issuing (exporter's) bank in a L/C transaction; also known as the notifying bank.
Affreightment	A written agreement by which a ship's owner agrees to rent out a ship or part of a ship to a shipper for the carriage of freight.
Agent	A person or firm authorized by the seller, known as the principal, to enter into binding contracts of sale on the seller's behalf (see Distributor). An agent represents the exporter and does not take title.
Applicant	The party applying for a L/C, usually the importer or buyer of the goods specified in the sales contract.
Arbitrage	Simultaneous buying and selling of foreign currencies to make a profit from discrepancies between exchange rates prevailing at the same time in different locations.
Arbitration	A dispute resolution mechanism that entrusts the settlement of an international trade dispute to an independent person or persons (arbitrators) under an arbitration clause in the contract signed by the parties involved. A resulting arbitral award can be enforced by a court.
Asset efficiency	A financial ratio that measures a firm's profitability, calculated by dividing sales by total assets, and expressed as total asset turnover (the number of times assets are turned over in one year). Asset efficiency multiplied by profitability of sales equals the percentage return on assets.
ATA Carnet (admission temporaire - temporary admission)	An international customs document issued by the importing nation's chamber of commerce for the temporary duty-free importation of certain goods into a country in place of the usual required customs documents and import duties.
Average collection period	A financial ratio calculated by dividing a firm's accounts receivable turnover into 365 days.

Average days in inventory	A financial ratio calculated by dividing inventory turnover into 365 days.
Balance of payments (BOP)	A financial statement which reports all payment transactions between residents of one country and those of all other countries, usually over a one-year period, comprising the current account, the capital account, and the official reserves account.
Beneficiary	The exporter, or the seller, who receives payment from a bank under a L/C set up by the importer, or buyer.
Bill of exchange	A negotiable instrument; an unconditional written order signed by one party (the drawer) and addressed to another (the addressee), requiring the addressee to pay a sum of money to the drawee, who becomes the acceptor by writing its name (to indicate acceptance) across the bill. A cheque is a simple form of bill of exchange, in Canada, usually known as a draft.
Bill of lading (B/L)	The primary trade transport document required to help ensure the security of goods shipped by an exporter. Sent to a foreign bank, it authorizes the bank to release the goods to the buyer only when payment has been received. It serves as 1) the carrier's receipt to the shipper that the goods have been received for shipment, 2) a memorandum of the terms and conditions of the contract between the carrier and the shipper for the transportation of the goods to a specified destination, and 3) evidence of title to the goods. A B/L may be negotiable or non-negotiable; various types include air bill, ocean bill, highway pro-bill and rail waybill.
Business plan	An internal company management document which describes how the business intends to achieve its goals over time through the use of sales forecasts, expenses, profits, performance mileposts, major financial ratios, etc.; required with a financial proposal to a lender.
Buyer credit	A medium- to longer-term trade financing method, best suited to large-scale financing of major capital and turnkey projects. The funds are loaned directly to the foreign buyer, who enters into a direct financial relationship with the lending bank.
Cargo control document	An advice note, house bill or other approved document that lets customs know when a shipment has entered Canada. It controls the movement and disposition of the goods until they are released by customs.
Carrier	Any person or company that, under a contract of carriage, undertakes to perform or procure the carriage agreed to by rail, road, sea, air, inland waterway or by a combination of such modes.

Cash flow planning	The study of a company's cash revenues and disbursements to identify gaps that require financing. A cash flow statement is drafted before the start of the fiscal year, then revised and updated monthly to show actual performance.
Cash in advance	The payment method with the least risk for the seller, and the greatest risk for the buyer; prepayment.
Certificate of origin	A NAFTA export document showing that the specified goods presented at Customs originated in either the United States, Canada or Mexico, and are therefore entitled to the preferential NAFTA tariff.
Collateral	A security given in addition to the principal security in a loan transaction. For example, a person who borrows money on the security of a mortgage may be required to deposit shares with the lender as additional or collateral security.
Collection	A payment method in which the exporter ships the goods to the importer and mails the shipping documents to a collecting bank which obtains payment from the importer in exchange for the documents. The exporter holds title to the goods until payment is received.
Co-marketing	Promotion and sale of complementary products, in cooperation with an established player in a target market, for a fee or percentage of sales; one of a number of cooperative business approaches used by smaller companies, including joint ventures, strategic alliances, research consortiums, licensing, franchising, and co-production; also known as piggyback marketing.
Common carrier	Any means of transporting goods, whether by sea, rail, air or road where the service must be offered to all legitimate users.
Competitive advantage	A positive quality or particular strength that places a company ahead of others in the industry (e.g. unique assets, processes or products, employee skills, business partnerships, size and reputation); also, a feature in a product or service that is perceived as a benefit by the buyer (e.g. price, exchange rate, image, advertising); also, known as differentiation or point-if difference.
Conference carriers	An association of shipping lines that offers a common set of rates for the movement of commodities and a fixed (usually weekly) sailing schedule.
Consolidation	A grouping together of several separate shipments by a consolidator or freight forwarder. The shipment is then shipped to an agent or de-consolidator under one bill of lading and reported to customs agents on one cargo control document.

Contract	A written or oral promissory agreement between two or more persons to do a particular activity or enter into a relationship that is enforceable by law.
Co-production	An offset transaction for overseas production based on a government-to-government agreement that permits a foreign government or a producer to acquire the technical information and know-how to manufacture all or part of an item.
Cost-based pricing	Price-setting method that uses all of the costs incurred in a transaction to set the final price; the most common include domestic costs plus mark-up, full-cost and marginal cost.
Costing analysis	A basic step in the financial plan for an export sale, it is used to predict the outflow of cash during the course of the transaction and test its profitability.
Cost-plus pricing	A method to calculate the export price of an item that starts with the domestic price, eliminates non-applicable domestic costs like promotion, and adds exporting costs such as transportation and insurance.
Credit character	The buyer's willingness to pay and otherwise meet its commercial obligations under the commercial contract.
Cross rates	The expression of a foreign exchange rate in terms of both currencies. Thus to say "the US dollar is worth $1.359 in Canadian funds, and the Canadian dollar $0.735 in US funds," is to give the cross rates for the two currencies.
Cross-licensing	A strategic partnership between two firms for the purpose of licensing products or services to each other in order to share products and expertise to their mutual benefit (see Licensing agreement).
Currency risk	The possibility of financial loss inherent in the fluctuations in the exchange rate between the Canadian dollar and the currency the parties choose for the settlement of their transaction; also known as foreign exchange risk (see Risk assessment).
Current ratio	A financial measure of liquidity, or how easily a business can meet its current debts, calculated by dividing current assets by current liabilities.
Customs broker	A trade professional who provides customs services including the processing of customs, import and export documents, and the release of commercial goods through the local customs authority.

Debt servicing	In a company's financial plan or financial proposal to a lender, a clear statement of how the borrowed funds and interest are to be repaid to the lender, on the basis of the expected income less projected costs, and the precise timing of the repayment.
Debt servicing ratio	A measure of net revenue earned for each dollar paid to service debt calculated on the basis of a formula involving company earnings, payment of debt principal and interest, and the marginal tax rate.
Defensive interval	The number of days of projected operating expenses that are covered by a company's cash, accounts receivable and merchandise holdings.
Direct exporting	A sale done without any intermediaries by an exporter to a buyer in a foreign country.
Dispute	Disagreement or conflict over provisions of a contract agreement, resolved by mediation, arbitration or court action.
Distribution	The movement of goods and services from the manufacturing process through to delivery to the customer. Logistics is defined as physical distribution plus materials management (see Logistics).
Distribution channels	The three major links between the seller and the final buyer. The first is the seller's marketing headquarters, where decisions on international channels and marketing mix are made. The second is made up of channels between countries and delivers the product to the border of the country; it can include agents, trading companies, means of transportation, financing, insurance, etc. The third comprises channels within the foreign country, or in-channels, and moves the product from the border entry point to the final buyer; it can include wholesalers.
Distributor	A purchaser of goods from a seller or exporter for purposes of resale on its own account; differs from an agent in that a distributor takes title to the goods and is the exporter's customer. A distribution agreement will be made between the exporter and the distributor. (see Agent).
Economies of scale	Savings due to a large production capacity, enabling a factory or an industry to manufacture large quantities of a product with the greatest efficiency and at the lowest price. Also known as economies of mass production.
Electronic Data Interchange (EDI)	A computer-to-computer system that transmits information and documents without human intervention.
Exclusivity	A clause in a contract that gives an agent, licensee or franchisee sole rights, within a defined territory, to represent a manufacturer, distribute a firm's product or service, or use an intellectual property; also, a company's sole right to a registered trademark.

Flexible pricing strategy	The sale of the same product to different classes of customers at different prices (see Pricing strategy).
Freight forwarder	A shipping industry professional who provides the exporter with a range of support services. These include advising on transportation of freight; selecting the best route and means of transport; arranging safe and cost-effective transport of the goods; and attending to all customs formalities and shipping documentation.
Indirect exporting	Sale by an exporter to a foreign buyer through an intermediary based in the exporter's country. These intermediaries can include commission agents, EMCs or trading houses, marketing boards, or buying agents for foreign governments.
Intermediary	Any party that acts as a go-between in an export transaction, including a broker, a freight forwarder, an agent, etc.
Joint venture	A form of business partnership involving joint management and the sharing of risks and profits. If joint ownership of capital is involved, the partnership is known as an equity joint venture; if it is an unincorporated venture set up for a short time and a limited undertaking, it is a contractual joint venture sometimes called a consortium; such a joint venture is similar to a partnership.
Just-in-time (JIT)	A computerized method of production initiated by and tailored to customers' needs and wants. Pioneered in Japan after World War II, JIT methods were designed to eliminate the need for raw material inventories. Instead, raw materials are delivered to the assembly line in a factory "just in time" to be assembled into the final product. This eliminates the waste and cost of huge inventories and enhances product quality.
Letter of Credit (L/C)	A document issued by a bank at the request of the buyer promising to pay the seller an agreed amount of money upon receipt by the bank of certain documents within a specified time.
Licensing agreement	A business arrangement under which a firm transfers the rights to the use of its product or service (or proprietary rights over certain technology, trademarks, etc.) to one or more firms in return for specified royalties or other payment (see Cross-licensing).
Litigation	The action of suing someone in a court of law for the purpose of enforcing a right, seeking redress, etc.

Logistics	The management and physical distribution of goods and materials. Individual services include purchasing, production planning, inventory control, materiels handling, warehousing, transportation, order processing, and customer service. Logistics professionals include carriers, freight forwarders, customs brokers, warehouse operators, distributors, couriers, purchasing agents, and inventory and materiel managers (see Distribution).
Market entry	The establishment of a presence in the foreign target market.
Market maintenance	Holding down prices to maintain market share despite increased pricing strategy costs (see Pricing strategy).
Market research	The systematic study of the foreign target market to establish its receptivity to a product or service. The country's economic and socio-political environment, the particular industry and economic sector, as well as all competitors, must be thoroughly reviewed through the use of techniques such as polls and surveys, focus groups, analyses of census and other published demographic and economic data, etc.
Market skimming	Charging premium prices to selected segments of the market to maximize profits from a relatively low sales volume (see Pricing strategy).
Marketing plan	Strategy and implementation steps for promoting and selling a product or service in the target market.
Marking and labeling	Special handling instructions or symbols printed on a package for shipping purposes. Also known as "lead marks" or "marks and numbers."
Materiels management	The supervision of materials from the supplier to the end of the production line.
Mode of transportation	The carrier that takes a shipment of goods to its destination. Usually done by truck, plane, ship, train and/or pipeline.
Offer and acceptance	The negotiating sequence of proposal and assent to that proposal, which may lead to an agreement. The one to whom the offer is made may accept it unconditionally, accept it with conditions, reject it or make a counteroffer. Under the Vienna Convention, revocation of an offer must reach the offeree before or at the same time as the offer. Where an irrevocable offer was made, however, no revocation is possible.
Partnership	An unincorporated business operated by two or more people with a view to profit. Taxed like a sole proprietorship, debt liability risk to the partners is unlimited. In a limited partnership, one or more of the parties participate as a passive partner.

Penetration	The use of low prices to capture market share
Pricing analysis	A detailed study of the cost elements of a product or service to determine the export price. A basic step in the financial planning for an export sale, it is used to predict expected revenues from the transaction and thus determine whether the company's products are competitive in the target market.
Pricing strategy	The planned pricing approach within the overall marketing strategy for the target market; traditional strategies include flexible, static, penetration and value-based pricing, market maintenance, and price skimming.
Primary research	Market studies conducted for a specific project through direct observation, questionnaires and interviews.
Proper law of the contract	The system of law by which an international contract is to be interpreted.
Risk assessment	A detailed study to identify the possibilities of financial loss in an export sale as a result of default by the buyer (commercial risk), political circumstances in the buyer's market (country or political risk), or exchange rate fluctuations in foreign currency markets (currency or foreign exchange risk).
Rules of origin	NAFTA regulations that determine to what extent goods that contain foreign components or materials are eligible for free trade status, i.e. reduced tariff rates.
Sale of goods	A contract between a buyer and a seller whose terms state that the seller, in consideration for the payment or promise of money, will transfer ownership and possession of goods to the buyer.
Secondary research	Market studies that have already been conducted and are available from conventional library, electronic or other sources.
Static pricing strategy	The charging of one price to all customers for a given product (see Pricing strategy).
Strategic alliance	An arrangement whereby one company cooperates, joins or works with another company to become more efficient or increase market share.
Technology transfer	Acquisition of technology from abroad, usually by one of several means, including licensing, joint ventures, limited R&D partnerships, contracts with or a minority interest in R&D firms, contracts with research institutes or universities, technological intelligence, or outright purchase of the company that owns the technology.

Title	The right to a property, considered either in terms of the way that right was acquired or its capacity to be effectively transferred. A title may be original, as with a patent or copyright, or derivative, where the person entitled takes the place of a predecessor by agreement of the parties or under a law, as when a buyer receives the purchased goods.
Trade barriers	Difficulties to be overcome by the exporter in penetrating the target market. These can be physical (distance, geography, climate, poor transportation systems); political and regulatory (instability, protectionism, currency restrictions, complex documentation requirements), systemic (electrical, safety standards, etc.), cultural (language, local practices, tastes and preferences) or due to corrupt and inefficient business cultures.
Trading house	A firm engaged in importing, exporting, and third-country trading in goods and services manufactured or provided by another company. Trading houses provide a variety of services, including assistance with shipping documentation, freight forwarding, etc.
Truckload (TL)	A transportation term used when a small shipment, either less-than-truckload (LTL) or less-than-carload (LCL), is consolidated into a full load to obtain preferred rates.

Appendix 6: Most Commonly-Used Incoterms

Negotiated term	Exporter's obligation	Additional costs assumed by exporter
EXWorks (EXW)	Ends at the factory loading dock	▪ none
Free Carrier (FCA)	Ends when the goods are delivered to the carrier's facility, i.e. when delivering goods for container stuffing	▪ loading at factory ▪ insurance ▪ inland transport
Free Alongside Ship (FAS)	Ends at the dock of the port of lading	▪ loading at factory ▪ insurance ▪ inland transport ▪ unloading at dock
Free on Board (FOB)	Ends when goods placed on the ship	▪ loading at factory ▪ insurance ▪ inland transport ▪ unloading at dock ▪ loading onto vessel
Cost and Freight (CFR)	Pays cost/freight of transporting goods to the port of destination	▪ loading at factory ▪ insurance ▪ inland transport ▪ unloading at dock ▪ loading onto vessel ▪ freight and other charges ▪ additional documentation ▪ freight forwarder's fees

Negotiated term	Exporter's obligation	Additional costs assumed by exporter
Cost, Insurance, Freight (CIF)	Pays cost/freight of transporting goods to the port of destination, and obtains insurance against the buyer's risk of loss	<ul><li>loading at factory</li><li>insurance</li><li>inland transport</li><li>unloading at dock</li><li>loading onto vessel</li><li>freight and other charges</li><li>additional documentation</li><li>freight forwarder's fees</li><li>marine insurance</li></ul>
Delivered Duty Paid (DDP)	Responsible for goods, including customs clearance, until shipment reaches the specified destination in the importing country	<ul><li>loading at factory</li><li>insurance</li><li>inland transport</li><li>unloading at dock</li><li>loading onto vessel</li><li>freight and other charges</li><li>additional documentation</li><li>freight forwarder's fees</li><li>marine insurance</li><li>unloading fees</li><li>duties</li><li>customs broker's fees</li><li>transportation</li><li>loading and unloading charges</li></ul>

Note: There are 13 Incoterms altogether. See **www.iccwbo.org/index_incoterms.asp** for detailed information about all of them.

Appendix 7: Illustration of Incoterms

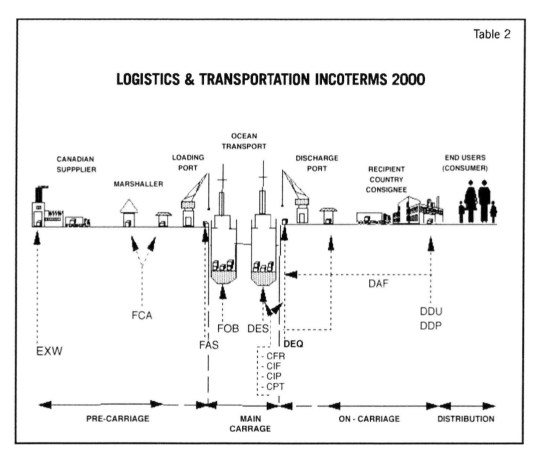

Table 2

LOGISTICS & TRANSPORTATION INCOTERMS 2000

Source: **www.acdi-cida.gc.ca/cida_ind.nsf/0/bd49664819a53ed7852568850065b94d?OpenDocument#sec12**

Index

A

B

C

D

E

F

G

I

M

N

O

P

Q

R

S